How to Get a Civil Service Job: Your Guide to a Government Career

Margaret Peter

How to Get a Civil Service Job: Your Guide to a Government Career

© 2018 Margaret Peter All rights reserved.

No portion of this book may be reproduced in any form without permission from the author, except as permitted by U.S. copyright law.

Cover by Go On Write at https://www.goonwrite.com

Table on Contents

Introduction	9
Why is it So Hard to Get a Civil Service Job?	11
• Getting a Private Sector Job vs. a Government Job	11
• Sample Timeline to get a Government Job	15
Why Work for the Government?	18
• Government Benefits	18
The Civil Service Workforce	20
• What Kind of Work Will You Do?	20
• How Many Government Employees Are There?	22
• What Kind of Jobs Are There?	22
• Where Are These Jobs?	28
The Benefits of Working for the Government	30
• Job Security	30
• Older Workers Welcome	31
• Diverse Workforce	33
• No Discrimination	36
• You Don't Need a College Degree	38
• Equal Pay	39
• Ability to Promote	40
• Professional Membership	40
• Many Careers, One Employer	41
• Union Membership	41
• Job Satisfaction	43
• Work-Life Balance	45

- Teleworking 46
- Guaranteed Employment 47
- Job Training and Promotion 48
- Low Cost Commuting 48
- Parking Program 49
- Discounts 49
- Public Service Loan Forgiveness 50
- Travel Reimbursement 51

Salary 52
- Differential Pay 53
- Negotiating a Higher Pay 54

Retirement 56
- Pensions 56
- Early Retirement 59
- Retire a Millionaire 60
- 401(k) and 457 Plans 61

Health Insurance 62
- Health Insurance Options 62
- Medical and Dependent Reimbursement Accounts 62
- Vision Insurance 63
- Dental Insurance 64
- Long Term Care Insurance 64
- Long Term Disability Insurance 65
- Legal Services 65
- Employee Wellness Programs 66

Vacation and Other Time Off 68
- Vacation 68
- Sick Leave 69

- Holidays — 70
- Voluntary Time Off — 71
- Family and Crisis Leave — 71
- Sabbatical Leave — 72
- Mentoring Leave — 73
- Donation Leave — 73
- Catastrophic Leave — 74
- Military Leave — 74
- FMLA — 75
- Parental Leave — 76
- Jury Duty — 77
- Time Off to Vote — 77

The Challenges of Government Employment — 78
- Will You Succeed as a Civil Worker? — 78
- Challenge #1: Why is the Salary So Low? — 80
- Challenge #2: Why is There So Much Red Tape? — 81
- Challenge #3: Why Do I Have to Act Like Everyone Else? — 82
- Challenge #4: Why Am I the Only One Doing the Work? — 84
- Challenge #5: Why Do I Have to Work with Idiots? — 85
- Challenge #6: Why Does My Boss Seem to Hate Me? — 86
- Challenge #7: Why Do I Feel Like I'm Part of the Problem? — 88

Getting Hired — 90
- How Does the Hiring Process Work? — 90
- Step #1: Apply to Take an Exam — 90
- Step #2: Take the Exam — 91
- Step #3: Get Your List Results — 92
- Step #4: Apply for Vacant Positions — 93

- Step #5: Interview   93
- Step #6: Pass Probation   94

Step #1: Apply to Take an Exam   95
- Why an Exam?   95
- How Exams Work   96
- The Life Cycle of an Exam   97
- Types of Exams   99
- Finding an Exam   101
- How Long Do Exams Stay Open?   102
- How to Read an Exam Bulletin   103
- How Will I Know What Exam is Being Given?   104
- Am I Qualified to Take the Exam?   105
- Applying to Take the Exam   106
- What If You're Not Admitted to the Exam?   108
- Tips to Filling Out the Exam Application   108
- Internet Exams   110
- Qualifications Exams   111
- Disability Accommodations   114

Step #2: Take the Exam   116
- Exam Scoring   116

Step #3: Get Your List Results   117
- What Happens After You Take an Exam   117
- Your Ranking   120
- Challenging an Exam Score   121
- Exam List Expiration Date   121
- If You Scored in Rank 1…   122
- What's an "Employment Inquiry" Letter?   124

Step #4: Apply for Vacant Positions   126
- What's on the Application?   127

- Filling Out the Application — 128
- Proofread Your Application — 130
- Cover Letters and Resumes — 131
- Submit Your Application — 132

Step #5: Interview — 125
- What a Government Job Interview is Like — 137
- Clean Up Your Digital Image — 139
- Sample Interview Questions — 140
- Interview Tips — 141
- What is the Interview Panel Looking For? — 142
- The Ideal Candidate — 144
- Ask a Question at the End — 145
- What Happens After the Interview — 146
- The Reference Check — 147
- If You Didn't Make the Cut — 148
- How Many Interviews Does it Take to Get a Government Job? — 149

Step #6: Pass Probation — 150
- What if You Don't Get Offered the Job You Want? — 150
- Picking Your Start Date — 151
- Choosing Your Working Hours — 151
- What is Probation? — 152
- Passing Your Probation — 157
- If You're Having Problems on Probation — 158
- File a Grievance — 158
- Weingarten Rights — 160
- Personnel File — 162
- After Probation — 164

FAQ — 165

About the Author — 176

Introduction

Congratulations. If you're reading this, you've taken a step towards getting a civil service job.

In this book, you'll be getting advice from someone who walks the walk and talks the talk. I have worked for the government for almost fifteen years. But it wasn't easy to get that first job.

My first attempts to get a civil service job were painful, filled with struggles, and ended nowhere. I knew that civil service jobs had good benefits – but I had no idea how to get one. I tried applying to my local county, city, and even the state, but I couldn't figure the purpose of exams and why I couldn't just apply for a job directly. This was before the internet. The only information I could glean was from calling local employment boards – calls that always ended up going to someone's voicemail, and which were never returned.

After about a year of trying, I succeeded in getting myself registered to take an in-person exam for an Office Assistant. I took the exam, and passed. But I never got contacted with offers of employment. At the time, I didn't understand that I needed to be very proactive about applying for jobs, and that no one would contact me for a job.

Eventually, I went to back to college as a slightly older student. During that time, I began my career in civil service as a student assistant for a government agency. After several years of working as a student, I took the exam for Office Technician and was hired as a full-time, fully benefited government employee. Since then, I have taken new exams and promoted into higher positions every few years. I have worked for a variety of government agencies, and I currently work in a salaried, high-level position.

This guide provides everything you need to know about getting a civil service job. Although there may be changes over time, the civil service employment process has remained consistent for decades. No matter when you're reading this book, you should get some good information from it.

In addition to providing the steps necessary to getting the job, this guide contains information about acclimating yourself to the government work culture. If you have worked for the private sector, especially for a long time, you may find it especially difficult to understand how job performance in government work is evaluated. You may rebel at the bureaucratic processes which are everywhere in government employment. You'll need to learn to adjust to a new way of working in order to keep your job.

Happy job hunting!

Why is it So Hard to Get a Civil Service Job?

99% of people who want a government job will never get one.

That's the sad reality. Competition for government jobs are fierce. The average vacant position announcement for an entry-level government job gets over 200 applications. A lot of people who want a government job never even make it to the stage where they *can* submit an application!

Welcome to the civil service process. If you're not familiar with the process, it can be a shock.

Getting a Private Sector Job vs. Government Job

In the private sector, these are the steps that you typically take to get a job:
1. Search for job postings online, through social media, in the newspaper, or word of mouth.
2. Find a job that you like.
3. Email your resume.
4. Either get a rejection letter or a phone call offering an interview.
5. Interview, typically with one person.
6. Get the job offer.
7. Start working.

The civil service process goes something like this:
1. Locate the civil service name for the type of job you want to do.
2. See if there is an exam currently being offered.
3. If not, wait for the exam to be offered (can take up to 3 years.)
4. Take the exam.
5. Wait to be notified of the results.
6. If you did not "rank" high enough, typically wait one year to take the exam again.
7. If you have "ranked" high enough, search for job postings for this position.
8. Mail your application package before the vacancy date closes.
9. Either get rejection letter, or a phone call offering an interview.
10. Interview, typically with a panel.
11. Get the job offer.
12. Start working.

Starting to get a little overwhelmed already? Most people give up before they even get to the interview stage.

Ironically, this is exactly what the civil service system is designed to do.

Are there enough government jobs for everyone that wants one?

No! The civil service employment process is one giant gatekeeping system. It is designed to keep you out. And it does just that. It keeps 99% of the applicants out. Eventually, most applicants give up, convinced that you need to "know someone" to get a job.

Most people give up in the first few weeks. The applicants who are willing to spend a year – or more – to get a job usually get one.

The civil service process also has a steep learning curve. Most people are not used to dealing with an employer who doesn't want to personally communicate with them. The government is large, bureaucratic, slow to respond, and hard to understand. There are hundreds of agencies, and thousands of job postings. It's like running around in a giant maze.

Most people also struggle with the concept of needing to take an exam to get a job. For most people, the last time they took a test was in high school, or maybe college.

If that's not enough, the exams can be confusing, too. It's not a one-size-fits-all exam. Exams take many forms. All of the following examples are civil service exams:
- an online test in which you self-select you own level of knowledge and skills (basically, a multiple choice test where you indicate how qualified you are)
- an oral examination (just like an interview)
- a series of essay questions

- a more traditional exam given in a room and proctored by a government employee, with an additional requirement that you obtain a typing certificate from an approved vendor on your own

Once you have applied for and successfully taken an exam - and assuming that you score high enough that you are considered "reachable"- only then you can start the process of applying for jobs.

Searching for a government job can also be a bit of a process. You can search for jobs by the following parameters:
- Keyword
- Job title
- Agency
- Geographical location
- Tenure (permanent, limited term)
- Timebase (full time, part-time, intermittent)
- Minimum and maximum salary (monthly, not annually)

Every step of the way in civil service employment, you are presented with confusing information – or too much information. It is hard to get an overall picture of how someone actually gets a job. It is very easy to miss a step, or apply for the wrong kind of job, or get lost and give up. This is all by design.

As I said earlier, there are many more applicants than there are jobs, and the easiest way to get less applicants is to make the process as confusing as possible!

Sample Timeline to Get a Government Job

Getting a government job takes much more time than in private sector. Here is a sample timeline:

January 1st: Your New Year's Resolution is to get a government job. You go to the official website for your local city/county/government/federal Jobs Board. You find hundreds – maybe even thousands - of positions listed. Overwhelmed, you read through all of the material on the website – which takes hours. You finally understand that first you need to look at "open" exams before you can apply for a job.

January 5th: You locate an "open" exam for a job you are interested in.

January 8th: You apply to take the exam.

January 23rd: Exam listing closes.

February 16th: You receive a letter saying you are qualified to take the exam; your exam is scheduled for March 6th.

March 6th: Take exam.

March 29th: You receive a letter saying you passed the exam; you are "reachable" in Rank 3.

April 1: You begin searching for vacant job postings.

April 4th: You send out your first standardized form for a job application. You sent it in response to a particular job listing.

April 23rd: The vacancy for this particular job listing closes.

May 6th: You are called and asked to participate in an interview.

May 18th: You interview with a panel of 3 people.

May 31st: You either get a call from HR, or you call HR yourself and find out they have selected another candidate.

June 6th: You realize that getting a government job is a numbers game. You begin applying for several positions every week.

June through September: You have 5 more interviews.

September through November: You have 6 more interviews.

November 20thst: An HR department requests you to provide your references.

November 22th: Your references are called. One of your references is traveling for Thanksgiving. They take a week to return the phone call.

December 5th: You are offered a job, with a start date of January 2nd.

Congratulations! It took you about a year to get the job.

Is it the same amount of time for everyone?

Not at all.

The fastest that I have heard of someone getting a government job, from start to finish, was 4 months. The longest I have heard of was a little over 2 years.

Other government workers have shared with me what it took to get their jobs. The typical "success story" had to do a lot just to get that first job offer. The average government worker I spoke to had:
- Eligibility on 1 to 4 different exam lists
- 100 – 200+ applications submitted
- 6 – 25 interviews

This is assuming that you have had some college – though not necessarily a degree - and prior office experience.

If you have a very specific, high-skill career – doctor, dentist, chaplain, psychiatrist, etc. – you are eligible for unique exams that have very little competition and you may find employment much faster.

Why Work for the Government?

With how hard it is to get a government job, why bother at all? What makes a government job worth it?

There are some "big ticket" benefits that you've likely heard about. These would be things like a pension, health care, and that you will have a job for life.

Government Benefits

But there are also dozens of other, small benefits.

Benefits like:
- The "dignity clause" – a requirement in most union contracts that your employer treat you with respect and dignity
- Weingarten rights – based off of the case of *NLRB v. J. Weingarten* – which gives employees the right to have union representation at investigatory interviews
- Reimbursement for professional memberships, workshops, and training
- Access to legal services, group insurance, long-term care insurance, free counseling, etc.
- Sabbatical leave

- Time off for mentoring, blood donation, and voting
- Discounts on public transportation or pre-tax parking benefits

Depending on whether you work for the city, county, government, or the feds, your benefits will be different.

However, it is safe to say that most government employees enjoy the following benefits:
- 40 hour work week
- Work week that is Monday – Friday, business hours, and with weekends off
- Plenty of training as you start your job
- Continuous, ongoing training in order to keep your skills fresh - whether through seminars, webinars, or conferences
- Progressively more time off – more vacation and sick leave as you work more years in civil service
- Injury or death compensation
- FMLA leave
- Health care, dental care, vision care
- Pension and/or 401(k)

One of the biggest benefits is that you will be working for one of the largest, most secure, and most financially stable entities in the United States. The U.S. government is *the* largest employer in the United Governments. About 1 in 6 working people in the U.S. are employed by some branch of the government.

And the good news is…the government is always hiring.

The Civil Service Workforce

Who is a civil service worker?

A civil service worker is anyone employed directly by the government, at any level. This could be on a federal level, government level, or city, county, or township level.

This book is designed to cover the general principles of civil service employment. No matter what level you are applying at, you should have some idea of what to expect in regards to the employment process, benefits, and professional culture.

What Kind of Work Will You Do?

Civil service generally employs two categories of workers:
- Professional
- Trade, crafts, or labor

Within these categories, there are hundreds of different jobs in civil service. In every category you could think of.

For example, some of the different categories are:

Professional (higher level, graduate degree level)
- Administrative (Bachelor's degree, office experience)

- Law Enforcement (from prison guards to professionals with a degree in Criminal Justice)
- Technical (computer technology related)
- Clerical (lower level, paraprofessional, only a high school degree required)
- Skilled trade (machine operators, maintenance and repair)
- Basic (skills such as custodial, laundry, etc.)

Who do you work for? When you're a civil service employee, you may work for any of the following employers:

- Agencies
- School districts
- Government offices
- Departments
- Commissions
- Boards
- Councils
- Hospitals
- Courthouses
- Attorney offices
- Welfare departments
- Water districts
- Public utilities
- Transportation systems
- Law enforcement
- Social services
- Employment services

No matter who you are, what your skill level is, how high your education level is, what your interests are, or where you live, you can get a job working for the government.

How Many Government Employees Are There?

Overall, there are about 22,000,000 government employees. 12% are federal, 24% are government, and 64% are at the local level.

In any given year, the government has an employee turnover rate of 10 to 15%. On average, they hire 2,200,000 to 3,300,000 new workers a year.

Why do so many workers leave government employment? They either quit, promote into higher-level government jobs, or retire.

Baby boomers account for a lot of turnover. Between the years 2015 and 2030, Baby Boomers are expected to retire – nationwide - at a rate of 10,000 people per day!

What Kind of Jobs Are There?

Government jobs are comprised of literally thousands of different job classifications and hundreds of different federal, government, and local agencies.

The kind of work that these employees do varies. A government employee can be a custodian, a file clerk, a park ranger, or a museum guide. Or, more commonly, a government employee can be an hourly employee who performs semiprofessional tasks in an office. An employee can also be a highly educated and salaried professional who directs an entire agency. Custodians, paper pushers, mid-level managers, assistants, and directors – the government hires them all!

All of the following people are government employees:
- Assistant who manages the professional and travel schedule of an Agency Director
- Custodian
- Physician who works with veterans
- Food service worker
- Lifeguard
- Researcher with a Ph.D. who writes reports for Congress
- Mail clerk
- Information Technology professional who runs an agency's Facebook and blog accounts
- Engineer who oversees the maintenance of the HVAC systems in several buildings
- Librarian who works in a prison
- Claims Examiner who processes claims for disabled police officers

Some positions require only a high school diploma or GED. Others require an undergraduate degree. Still, other positions require advanced professional education. No matter how educated you are – or aren't - all government workers get their jobs through some sort of qualifying education and/or experience.

Here's a universal truth: the government always needs workers. On all levels.

They need workers for a variety of fields. Generally, the government is always hiring in:
- Accounting
- Administration
- Budgeting
- Business
- Engineering and Sciences
- Environmental Services
- Finance
- Program Management
- Prison System
- Public Health
- Regulatory Compliance
- Research
- Transportation

Beyond that, there are some specific occupational areas that have been identified as having a large number of positions. According to the Bureau of Labor Statistic's Occupational Outlook Handbook, the top 25 positions in federal government employment are:

Top 25 Positions in Federal Government Employment

1. Miscellaneous clerks and assistants
2. Miscellaneous administration and program positions
3. Information technology management positions
4. Safety technicians
5. Nurses
6. Management and program analysis positions
7. Secretaries
8. Criminal investigators
9. General attorneys
10. Social insurance administrator positons
11. Contact representatives
12. Contracting positions, including contract officers and specialists
13. Air traffic controllers
14. General business and industry positions
15. General inspection positions, including investigators and compliance officers
16. Medical officers, including doctors
17. Human resources management positions
18. Electronics engineers
19. General engineers
20. Tax examining positions
21. Engineering technicians
22. General biological science positions
23. General education and training positions, including instructors and consultants
24. Correctional officers
25. Budget analysis positions

Interested in making as much money as possible in working for the government? Here are some of the highest paying jobs:

10 Highest Paying Government Jobs

1. Astronomer $116,072
2. Attorney $114,240
3. Financial Manager $101,022
4. General Engineer $100,051
5. Economist $94,098
6. Computer Scientist $90,929
7. Chemist $89,954
8. Criminal Investigator $88,174
9. Microbiologist $87,206
10. Architect $85,690

And here are some of the lowest paying jobs (which also have the lowest barrier to entry and require the least amount of skills):

10 Lowest Paying Government Jobs

1. Custodial Worker $33,140
2. General Student Trainee $32,305
3. Food Service Worker $31,958
4. Laundry Worker $31,925
5. Biological Science Trainee $30,890
6. Messenger $30,625
7. Personal Services $30,411
8. Agricultural Aide $28,203
9. Food Preparer/Server $26,918
10. Sales Store Clerk $22,026

Still not sure what job with the government that you would like to pursue? It's likely that you can find a job that matches your particular interests. For example, do you:
- **Love the arts?** …Work for the National Endowment for the Arts

- **Want to work with wildlife?** …Try the Department of Fish & Game, or Wildlife Conservation Board.
- **Love libraries?** … Work for the Library of Congress, or any number of government, city, or county library systems
- **Care about disability rights?** …Work for the U.S. Equal Employment Opportunity Commission, the U.S. Access Board, or the U.S. Department of Labor
- **Care about animals?** …Work for U.S. Fish & Wildlife or USDA Animal Care
- **Love the outdoors?** …Try U.S. National Park Service, or any number of government, county, or city parks
- **Care about the environment?** …Work for the U.S. Environmental Protection Agency, the National Oceanic and Atmospheric Administration, or the Department of Energy
- **Consider yourself a history buff?** …Work as a Historian in almost any federal or government agency, managing the agency's history files
- **Have an outgoing personality?** Work for the National Travel and Tourism Office
- **Want to help people?** …Go to the Department of Health and Human Services or the Department of Labor's Office of Disability Employment Policy
- **Want to work for a large agency?** Work the for the Department of Defense or the Department of Veteran's Affairs

- **Or, a small agency?** Try the National Capital Planning Commission or the Federal Retirement Thrift Investment Board

Where Are These Jobs?

You don't necessarily have to work in the nation's capitol to be employed by the government. About 87% of government jobs are located outside of Washington D.C. About 3% of government jobs are located abroad, in foreign countries.

Federal jobs, government jobs, city jobs, and county jobs can all offer you government employment.

Here is a list of the top ten areas that offer the highest number of federal jobs:

Top 10 Places to Get a Government Job

- Washington, D.C.
- California
- Texas
- Virginia
- Maryland
- Florida
- Georgia
- Colorado
- North Carolina
- New Jersey

Even in the smallest cities and towns, there is likely to be government work available.

The Benefits of Working for the Government

Nationwide, workers only stay with an employer for an average of 4.2 years.

Government employees, on the other hand, stay with their employer for an average of 20.4 years!

Why do workers stay in their government jobs so much longer than private sector workers?

Job Security

Government jobs are some of the most secure jobs in the world.

The government is not a corporation. That means that they don't need to show evidence of rising growth or profits to shareholders. Even better, no one is interested in a "corporate takeover" of the government. There is no need to "slash and burn" the payroll in order to produce a positive economic report!

When you're employed by the government, you don't have to fret every time there is a report of an economic downturn, or rising unemployment, or sign of a recession.

While other people may be constantly afraid of losing their job…you can have peace of mind throughout your entire career.

And if you do get laid off? Government employers are obligated to hire back their own laid off workers before they can make any other hire. Government employees are placed on a special "hire back" list that their government employer needs to empty before an "outside" (i.e., new to government service) hire can occur for any vacant positions.

In plainspeak: any employee who has been laid off, or who is in danger of being laid off, must be contacted and offered a job before anyone else gets a shot at it.

This is why a government job is truly a "job for life."

Older Workers Welcome

Age discrimination accounts for nearly ¼ of all complaints filed with the Equal Employment Opportunity Commission.

Well, good news! Age discrimination is not an issue when you work for the government. If you're age 40+, you're in good company!

According to the U.S. Office of Personnel Management, the average federal civilian employee is 47.5 years old.

Age discrimination is not a problem in government service.

Why? The government code, for starters.

The Age Discrimination in Employment Act (ADEA) forbids age discrimination against people who are age 40 or older.

Not only is age discrimination explicitly made illegal, the government has no reason to discriminate against you. No manager has a personal stake in hiring a younger candidate over an older candidate. It just does not matter to them.

I have heard stories about people as old as age 70 – yes, age 70! – getting government jobs.

But what if you're older AND disabled?

Again - the government doesn't care!

According to the U.S. Office of Personnel Management, 9.93% of federal employees are identified as having at least one disability.

Not only is there no age or disability discrimination, the government wants you even *after* you're retired!

Once you retire from your job, you can go back to work for the government in a position called "rehired annuitant." Some people work as retired annuitants for years. It's part-time work, which works well for most retirees.

Overall, this can be very lucrative option. You receive both an annuity and a salary.

A government job is an especially good deal for an older worker, because there is no age discrimination - and you get a pension.

But it's also a great fit for younger workers, too.

If you start working for the government when you're young, not only will you be able to retire up to fifteen years earlier than your peers, research suggests that you will be very fulfilled with your decision.

The Office of Personnel Management released a study on showing how Millennials (those born between 1981 and 1997) are the happiest government employees of any generation. Of those surveyed, 86% claim that they feel that their work is important, 83% claim that their bosses treat them with respect, and 66% feel that their bosses support their personal development.

Diverse Workforce

One of the benefits of working for the government is the diversity of your coworkers. You'll find that a government workforce is much more diverse than a corporate one.

According to the Office of Personnel Management, 36.68% of the federal workforce is made up of minorities. They are:

18.15% African American
8.75% Hispanic
5.99% Asian
1.69% Native American
0.51% Native Hawaiian/Other Pacific Islander

Women are also more represented in government civil service than the corporate world. They make up 43.38% of the government workforce.

To be clear, unfortunately discrimination *does* occur in the public sector, just as in the private sector…but public employees encounter it less.

Because potential job candidates are held to the standards of a civil service examination, what matters is how many points you score on the exam…not the color of your skin. Since so many of the exams take place remotely through the internet or by mailing in self-evaluating paperwork, a Human Resources manager never even sees you in person. They just score your exam, and move on to the next one. You are a piece of paperwork, not a person. You can't bias against paperwork.

Still worried about discrimination?

The government makes an effort to try to minimize discrimination. That's why government agencies have

Equal Employment Opportunity (EEO) programs and EEO officers.

EEO Officers are required to:

- Monitor, analyze, evaluate, and identify underutilization of employees by racial/ethnic, gender and disability categories
- Monitor, analyze, and report on the appointment of employees, and the composition of oral examination panels
- Eliminate illegal employment barriers
- Ensure no discriminatory employment practices, policies, or procedures exist within the work environment
- Have a written non-discrimination and harassment policy, procedures, and a dissemination process
- Conduct mandated sexual harassment prevention and education training

Here's all the ways that you *can't* be discriminated against in government service:
- Age
- Ancestry
- Color
- Disability (mental or physical)
- Gender
- Gender identity or expression
- Genetic information
- Marital status
- Medical condition
- Military veteran status
- National origin
- Political affiliation
- Pregnancy
- Race

- Religion
- Sex

Government agencies are required to undergo an annual analysis to determine whether a diverse group of employees are being represented in their workforce. If there is not sufficient enough diversity, the EEO Officer is required to work on improving the diversity of that agency's workforce.

No Discrimination

Government employees typically work with a union that guarantees that you will work in an environment that is free of discrimination, sexual harassment, and indignity.

Worried about age discrimination? As covered earlier, it's a non-issue.

Unlike a corporation, the government is *not* concerned about how much training and effort will be spent on someone who is 5-10 years away from retiring. Since roughly 10% of the government workforce quits, promotes up, or retires each year, the government must constantly hire new workers anyway, so it doesn't matter that they must constantly train new people.

Furthermore, corporations are famous for letting go of older, expensive workers and replacing them with younger, cheaper workers. But this is just not an issue in government service. Why?

Government pay is determined by position and range. It is *not* determined by what salary a young college graduate is willing to accept. All workers in the same classification get the same pay and benefits. All workers, regardless of age and experience, start at the beginning range – for example, Range A, or Step 1.

So far, so good. But what if you get a government job, and then you believe you're being discriminated against in your new job?

That's what the union is for. The union contact and the EEOC guarantees an environment "free of discrimination." If you think you are being discriminated against or harassed, you can file a grievance. Then you can pursue it with the Department of Fair Employment and Housing (DFEH), and/or the federal Equal Employment Opportunity Commission (EEOC).

But won't your boss "go after you" for filing a grievance? The union contract explicitly forbids retaliation, or threats of retaliation, from management or other workers. Alleged retaliation is subject to the grievance and arbitration procedures.

Worried about sexual harassment? You are guaranteed an environment free of sexual harassment. File a grievance.

Disabled? Worried about discrimination? Don't. The government is especially proactive about making sure that people with disabilities are not discriminated against. Many government agencies have a Disability Advisory Committee (DAC) made up of individuals with disabilities, or who have an interest in disability issues, to advise the head of the agency about concerns to employees with disabilities.

Many government employers also guarantee a right to be treated with dignity at work. Most employers also have some sort of Diversity Committee or a Workplace Violence and Bullying Prevention Program.

You Don't Need a College Degree

Want to work for the government without having to go to college first?

No problem.

Want to promote up without a college education?

No problem.

The government is one of the last workforces around that will hire you and promote you to an excellent wage with no more than a high school education. Many people start off at the lowest government positions possible – Office Clerk, Food Service Worker – and end their career as a manager, making six figures a year.

Equal Pay

Civil service salaries are gender-blind.

Salaries are very specific, and they have nothing to do with gender. The salary levels are created and outlined in labor contracts. Everyone gets the same salary, regardless of gender.

However, reports indicate that women in the government workforce earn about 79.5 cents on the dollar compared to men.

How can this be? Isn't this proof of discrimination?

Studies have shown that men have higher salaries because they're represented in greater numbers in the government's best-paying jobs. Jobs like: criminal justice officers, corrections officers, firefighters, engineers, computer programmers, attorneys, and physicians.

Female employees are more likely to occupy classifications that provided lower levels of compensation. Their male counterparts tend to be concentrated in mid-level to highly compensated classifications.

For example, here are two job classifications, broken down by gender:
- Mechanical and Construction Trades (91.2% are men)
- Office and Allied Services (77.6% are women)

Government officials want to address the wage gap by attracting female applicants in highly compensated classifications. It's a long-range goal that results in promotions and new hires.

Ability to Promote

Ever work for a company that has a "sink or swim" philosophy? Ever fail at a job because you couldn't catch on fast enough?

I have. Not a pleasant experience, is it?

The government is not like that. You are guaranteed to receive adequate training and to receive opportunities for advancement. Many government employers have written Upward Mobility Programs.

Many government employers even give you time paid off to take exams for other government jobs and to interview for other government positions, as long as these exams and interviews take place during your normally scheduled working hours.

Professional Membership

Does your job require you to be a member of a professional association? Then most government employers will pay for your membership!

They may not pay 100% of the cost of the membership, but most employers will at least pay a percentage of the dues or licensing fees.

Many Careers, One Employer

You can spend your entire career working for the government – and many people do.

Only when you are working for the government do you have the ability to try many different jobs - and career fields - without losing your benefits, or your primary employer.

Many people start off their government career in a relatively low position, such as Student Assistant, Office Assistant, Office Technician, or Mail Room Clerk. Over the course of their career, they switch jobs 4 or 5 times within government service, in order to end up in a senior position with much higher pay.

Union Membership

Government employees *who are not managers* are typically represented by a government union.

When you become a government employee, you automatically become what is called a "fair share" member. This means that you are entitled to the same protections as a "regular" member, but that you cannot run for a union position/office, and you cannot vote in union elections.

Fair share memberships typically cost around 99% of regular dues. The difference between being a "fair share" member and a "regular" union member can be as little as $1 a month.

As a union member, you are entitled to all the privileges and conditions as stated in the union's contract, also called the Master Agreement. This document – which is usually hundreds of pages long - spells out exactly what protections and rights government employees are eligible for.

One of the most practical benefits of being a part of the union is the ability to file a grievance. A grievance is a dispute between one or more employees – typically an employee and his or her manager. This dispute can be based on one of three things. One, it can be a disagreement between one of the rights in the contract. Two, it can be a dispute involving the application or interpretation of a written rule, such as a departmental rule, that does not explicitly appear in the contract. Three, it can be a complaint.

Grievances are primarily used by employees who feel that they are being treated unfairly by their manager.

Another interesting union benefit is the "Weingarten rights."

Weingarten rights refer to a statement that you can invoke at the time that your supervisor requests a meeting with you and you want union protection for whatever is about to occur in that meaning. Basically, if you think that your boss is about to discipline you, or even try to fire you, you would invoke you Weingarten rights. Say to your manager:

"If this discussion could in any way lead to my being disciplined or terminated, I respectfully request that my steward be present at the meeting before I answer any questions. Without representation present, I choose not to respond to any questions."

More information on grievances and Weingarten rights appear in the "Passing Probation" chapter.

Job Satisfaction

With government employment, you can find a job that uses your background, your skill set, and your interests. Hopefully, you will like your job for the government.

A recent Gallup poll found that 51% of employees said that were "not engaged" at work, and 17.5% were "actively disengaged."

That means that less than 1/3 of Americans actually like their jobs.

When you're working for the government, odds are good that you can find at least one job that can tolerate, or even like.

Surveys about government employee satisfaction have found that government employees typically describe their job as "challenging." Depending on how you interpret that word, that can either by a good thing, or a bad thing.

Other words that government employees have used to describe their jobs are:
- important
- stressful
- rewarding
- interesting
- busy
- demanding
- underpaid
- frustrating
- fun

There are good and bad things about government jobs. I will cover this more fully in the "Passing Probation" chapter.

However, I should mention that most people find government work meaningful. Why?

Rather than contributing to a company's bottom line, fattening a CEO's paycheck, or helping to propel a generation of shareholders to even greater wealth, your work provides services that are crucial to the well-being and functionality of the public.

Work-Life Balance

Welcome to the 40-hour work week!

Unless you are in a supervisor or management position for the government, odds are good that your working hours will be some variation of the standard 8 to 5. You won't work weekends, and you won't work overtime.

You can work for the government and still have a life. There's no pressure to be a superstar or an overachiever. You are not encouraged to get into the office 15 minutes early so you can have your computer up and all your necessary systems running when your shift begins. In fact, doing so is typically a violation of the union agreement. When you work for the government, the amount of time that it takes for you to turn on all your office equipment, get your first cup of coffee, and get settled in is all considered part of your work day.

There's no need to stay late, work late, or give up your weekends and miss another one of your kid's soccer games. Being a government employee guarantees you an appropriate work-life balance.

Never again will you have to stay late to show the boss what a productive worker you are. You won't have to get to work before sunrise, either. The union negotiates acceptable working hours and the usage of overtime. You will likely find that your manager is a stickler in making sure you get out the door on time – so that they don't accidentally have to pay you overtime!

If you don't have a job where you serve the public (meaning, you're not required to work 9am to 4pm in order to answer during the open hours of a public phone line or staff a public desk) you should also have some control over what your work hours are. If you don't want to work the standard 8 to 5, you can probably work some variant, like 7 to 3:30 to 9 to 6. You can take an hour lunch or a half hour lunch. Breaks are guaranteed, and encouraged.

You may also be able to get what is called an "alternative work schedule." This typically involves working nine-hour days in exchange for a Friday off every other week, or four 10-hour days a week for a Friday off every week. It does not change the number of hours worked, but simply allows each individual the flexibility to rearrange their work schedule to better meet their personal needs (while also considering the needs of the office.)

Teleworking

According to the American Community Survey, the typical American commutes for 52.8 minutes per day. Wouldn't it be nice to telework instead?

Telework is defined as: performing work one (1) or more days per pay period away from the work site to which the employee is normally assigned.

Some government employees have the option to telework. Some departments even have an official telework program. Employees work from home, logging into email and other systems remotely in order to complete their work.

After you get your first government job, check with your boss to see if telecommuting is a viable option for you. This option is usually reserved for higher level employees. Most managers have the option to telework.

Guaranteed Employment

If you get laid off from the government, the government is required to help you find another job within government service. They do this by placing you on a special list, typically called something like the Government Restriction of Appointment list.

You could call this the "laid off" list.

Another department with the same government entity, whether city, county, state, or federal, must hire employees from the "laid off" list before they can hire anyone else – especially "outside" employees (people that are brand new to government service.)

That means that if you are laid off, or you are in danger of being laid off, you must be contacted and offered a government job before any "outsider" gets a shot at that same job.

Job Training and Promotion

As a government employee, you are guaranteed adequate job training. Rather than the "sink or swim" work environment of a corporation, you are guaranteed to receive adequate training – and the ability to promote up.

If you don't, you can file a union complaint.

The government is typically very proactive about this. Most government agencies have some kind of Upward Mobility Coordinator in each agency to help their employees make the most of their careers.

Low Cost Commuting

If you use public transportation to get to work, many government agencies will subsidize the cost.

For example, in some agencies, government employees are eligible for a 75% discount on public transit passes, up to a maximum predetermined amount.

Similarly, employees riding in vanpools are eligible to receive up to a monthly reimbursement. The primary vanpool driver receives an even larger reimbursement.

Parking Program

If you work in a crowded metropolitan area that does not guarantee parking (such as a downtown area with metered parking or 2-hour parking spaces) some agencies have a Pre-Tax Parking Program. This is typically intended for government employees who don't have access to a government-controlled parking garage or parking program.

This is a voluntary payroll deduction program that allows you to deduct a specific dollar amount for work-related parking fees from your paycheck prior to tax deductions. In turn, this reduces your taxable income.

Discounts

When you're a government employee, you can typically get discounts on a wide variety of products and services. Check with your individual agency to see what you're eligible for.

One of the most well-known discounts is that you're eligible to receive a government rate on your cell phone. The discount can be substantial, saving you a large percentage each month.

Check with your carrier (AT&T, Verizon, etc.) to see if they offer this discount. You will need to provide you .gov email address so they can send a confirmation link to this email address before you get the discount.

Public Service Loan Forgiveness

Are you still paying off your student loans? Well, good news! You may qualify for the Federal Student Aid Public Service Loan Forgiveness Program.

The Public Service Loan Forgiveness (PSLF) Program forgives the remaining balance on your Direct Loans after you have made 120 qualifying monthly payments under a qualifying repayment plan while working full-time for a qualifying employer.

This program applies to federal student loans, such as:
- Any loan you received under the William D. Ford Federal Direct Loan Program
- Another other federal student loans such as the Federal Family Education Loan (FFEL) Program, and Federal Perkins Loan Program that have been consolidated into a Direct Consolidation Loan

Qualifying for the program is not automatic. After making your 120th qualifying payment, you will need to submit the PSLF application to receive loan forgiveness.

This program works best for students who have more than $30,000 in debt. For students who have less than $30,000 in debt, they are automatically funneled into a 120-payment repayment plan. These students do not exceed 120 payments, so they never become eligible for the program.

Travel Reimbursement

Government employees who incur authorized travel expenses related to official government business may apply for reimbursement for the following:

- Meals
- Incidentals
- Lodging
- Conference
- In Government Travel
- Out of Government Travel
- Out of Country Travel
- Personal Vehicle Mileage
- Public Transportation

Salary

Here's the section you've been waiting for: salary. I am sure that some of you may have skipped ahead to this chapter!

One of the first questions that potential government employees ask are: "How much money will I make?"

Government service runs the gamut of salaries.

This guide assumes that you are interested in an entry-level position. It also assumes that your education ranges between high school to some college.

These are some of the entry-level government service positions and their monthly salary ranges:

Accountant Trainee	$3,524 - $4,202
Administrative Assistant I	$3,977 - $5,210
Information Systems Analyst	$3,377 - $5,491
Governmental Program Analyst	$4,784 - $5,988
Custodian	$2,194 - $2,745
Office Assistant (General)	$2,255 - $3,195
Office Technician (General)	$2,868 - $3,593
Program Technician	$2,529 - $3,398
Staff Services Analyst	$3,063 - $4,980

For the record, the average annual government base salary is $84,913 (worldwide.)

Don't despair if your starting salary or your first entry-level position is far below that. Almost no one stays in an Office Assistant or Custodian position for life. You will likely promote up over the years, bringing your salary more in line with this number.

You will also receive a raise every year. It is most typically called a Merit-based Salary Adjustment (MSA) and it is generally an automatic raise. If it is ever denied to you, you can go to the union. 99% of government employees receive their MSA automatically.

Every year, you will get an MSA until you reach the top salary range or grade for your job classification.

After that, you will start to receive a Cost-Of-Living-Adjustment, also called a COLA. It is like a MSA, but it is a different percentage – usually less.

Differential Pay

When we're talking about salary, there's one easy way to earn extra money: work at night. If you have bilingual skills, that's another easy way to earn extra.

Government employees who regularly work the night shift may be eligible for extra pay, called a night shift differential.

Employees who are required to use a bilingual skill on a continuing basis for at least 10% of the time they are on their job may be eligible for extra pay, called bilingual differential pay.

Employees who are headquartered out of government, or who are on permanent assignment to travel at least 50% of the time out of the government may be eligible for extra pay, called out-of-government pay differential.

Once you become a government employee, check with your bargaining unit to see if you are eligible for any of these pay differentials.

Negotiating a Higher Pay

Can you negotiate a higher salary than the one posted for the job?

As already mentioned, a particular salary for a particular job has a range, or a grade. By default, you are started at the bottom of that range…unless you can give a compelling reason why you should be started higher.

For an idea about general salaries, look up the federal government's "General Pay Scale" or the pay ranges specific to the state, county, or city government agency that you are interested in.

So, once you have an idea what the starting salary is, how can you negotiate higher? What compelling reason can you present?

Employees are generally given a higher starting salary than the beginning of the range for one of these reasons:
- Years of experience
- You have specialized experience
- You have mission-critical skills
- The private sector job that you're quitting in order to take this government job pays you more than the government job, so you'll be taking a substantial paycut to work for the government
- You have received a job offer somewhere else that pays more
- You have travel and relocation expenses in order to take this job
- You be moving to an area with a higher cost of living in order to take this job

If you have one of those compelling reasons, and you can prove it (show them another job offer in writing, show them geographical information that shows your cost of living will go up substantially after you relocate, etc.) then you may be able to negotiate with the government HR team in order to start at a higher salary within the range or grade.

Retirement

One of the biggest benefits for working for the government is the retirement. Not only will you receive a pension, but you will also have the opportunity to contribute to a 401k and could get free medical insurance once you retire!

You can also retire early – sometimes decades ahead of your peers.

Pensions

Pensions (also called "Defined Benefit" plans) are rapidly becoming a thing of the past. U.S. companies have terminated more than 17,000 pension plans in the past 20 years. Currently, only 3% of American private-sector workers have a pension plan. But most public sector (government) employees have a plan.

Most pensions take at least 2 - 5 years to "vest." That means that you need to work for the government for that many years before you become "vested" in the pension system. If you leave before then, all of the money that was taken out of your account as retirement contributions will either be returned to you in one lump sum, or you can leave it in the government's 401k plan. But it will not be a pension.

Not all pensions are created equal. Due to the public backlash against pensions and concerns about pension funds running out of money, many new government employees are put in a different kind of pension plan than old-timers. These different pensions are usually referred to as "tiers." First-tier, second-tier, third-tier, etc. The further down the tier you go, the less generous your plan is. Government employees who have already worked for the government for a long time will be in tier-one. You may come in at tier-two or tier-three.

These second or third-tier programs are different in that:
- The minimum retirement age is higher
- Defined benefit percentage formula is less generous (you will receive less money)
- Safety members (meaning that you work in the correctional, fire, or police system) typically have a minimum retirement age of 50, which means that they must retire early

So, how do pensions actually work?

Your pension is based off three things:
1. Number of years you have worked for the government
2. How old you are when you retire
3. What your salary is

For each year that you work for the government, you earn 1 year of service credit. It accumulates on a fiscal year basis, from July 1 through June 30.

The older that you are when you retire, the more your benefit is multiplied. Your retirement will vary based on exactly who your government employer is, but in my research, I have discovered that it is generally sage to say that the employee who works until age 62 instead of retiring early at age 52 receives *double* the benefit of the employee who retired early.

This is also known as the "golden handcuffs" syndrome. You may want to retire early, but many employees don't because the longer they work, the more proportionately larger benefit they receive.

This is the nature of pensions. The pension system is betting that the older you are when you retire, the less they will have to pay out before you die. They want you to stay working longer, giving you less time to live in retirement. Older workers are rewarded with more significantly higher pension amounts because of their statistically shorter lifespan.

Another factor in determining your final pension amount, besides years of service, if your salary upon retirement. Your pension is typically based off of your highest three years of salary. Most government employees achieve this in the last few years of their career, as they accept positions as managers and department heads.

The *real* winners of the pension game are those who started government service later in life. The older you are when you start working for the government – in your 40's is ideal – the more generous your benefit will be when you retire.

Is there ever a point where you will receive 100% of your salary as a pension?

Yes. Under specific conditions, you can. For example, someone that starts working for the government at age 27 and retires at age 67 with 40 years of service will get 100% of their salary as a pension.

Early Retirement

Most people retire for the government after working for 20 years. The average is actually 20.4 years.

If you start working for the government in your 20's or 30's, you may find yourself retiring in your 50's or early 60's.

Once you have 20 or 30 years of service credit in with the government, you will receive a pension that enables you to retire in comfort. If you choose to work longer – see the "golden handcuffs" issue in the above section – your pension will become significantly larger with each year that you work. Still, many government employees retire on their 55th birthday.

If you're young – like a member of the Millennial or iGen – you will get a real benefit out of having a government job. Millennials hear constant recommendations that they should put aside 15% of each paycheck for their retirement, as soon as they get their first paycheck. When you work for the government, they automatically withdraw pension contributions from your paycheck – and it's a lot less than 15%! Decades later, these contributions are available as a generous pension that can fund an early retirement.

To further their money, many retirees choose to move to a government with no income tax or that offer special tax breaks to those with pension income. About 15% of those receiving government pensions choose to live outside of their home state once they retire. Popular cities for these retirees are: Las Vegas, Reno, Tucson, and Grants Pass. Some retirees have even moved to Puerto Rico and Guam.

Retire a Millionaire

Even if you don't end up collecting 100% of your salary as a pension, the benefits you receive will still be very generous – especially when you consider the current and future value of employee health insurance.

Research by the American Enterprise Institute (in their article "Not So Modest: Pension Benefits for Full-Career Government Employees") reveals that a full-term career government employee in the average government receives a retirement percentage that is equivalent to 87% of their final pay.

Furthermore, the average full-term government employee receives a lifetime retirement benefit with a present value of $768,940.

When you're a government employee, you can basically retire at the same level that a millionaire could. How can this be?

Government employees are "pension millionaires." That means that for many employees, the amount of money that they receive monthly from their pension is the same amount that a millionaire could withdraw from his or her account at a safe withdrawal rate.

Government employees also enjoy a cash equivalent value for the health insurance that they and their spouses receive in retirement. This can be a substantial amount of money!

In 2017, the Employee Benefit Research Institute issued a statement that a man would need to have $127,000 saved and a woman would need to have $143,000 saved in order to have a 90% chance of covering all of their healthcare costs in retirement. For a couple, that figure rises to $265,000. And for a couple with high prescription drug costs, it's $349,000.

When you retire with free or low-cost retiree health care from the government, this is like receiving a bonus worth somewhere between $127,000 and $349,000!

401(k) and 457 Plans

Many employers don't offer access to a 401k. The government does.

Employees typically may choose to contribute to a 401(k) Plan, a 457 Plan, or both. Some employees may also choose to contribute to a Roth 401(k). All contributions are transmitted through automatic payroll withdrawals, in amounts as little as $50 per month.

Health Insurance

Health Insurance Options

The government offers several different health care plans to choose from. These plans insure single parties, two-parties, and families. The government will pay a portion of your health insurance premium.

Although the plans are renegotiated every year, government employers typically include popular choices as: Anthem Blue Cross, Blue Shield, Health Net, Kaiser, United Healthcare, Western Health Advantage, PERS Choice, PERS Care, and special plans for correctional officers, police, and firefighters.

Typically, you have 60 calendar days from your first day to enroll in a health plan. Your health insurance will be start on the first of the month following the pay period in which your paycheck shows your employer contribution/insurance deduction.

Medical and Dependent Reimbursement Accounts

The government lets employees set aside money in a reimbursement account to pay for certain kinds of expenses. The employee specifies the amount to be deducted from their paycheck, and the deductions occur before tax withholding, thus reducing tax liability.

Currently, the government offers two kinds of accounts: Medical Reimbursement Accounts and Dependent Care Reimbursement Accounts.

A Medical Reimbursement Account lets you claim reimbursement for out-of-pocket medical services and/or supplies provided to you, your spouse, and your dependents if the services/supplies are related to:
- the diagnosis, cure, prevention, or treatment of a disease affecting any part or function of the body
- transportation primarily for and essential to this medical care

A Dependent Care Reimbursement Account is similar to a medical account except it is for paying daycare expenses. Expenses that qualify are:
- child care
- elder care and disabled dependent care

Vision Insurance

Government employees receive vision care. You are eligible for an eye examination, lenses, and a frame every calendar year.

The Basic Vision Plan is currently offered at no cost to government employees.

Dental Insurance

The government offers prepaid, indemnity, and PPO plans, such as DeltaCare or Delta Dental.

For the prepaid plans, the monthly premium is completely paid for by the government. For the other plans, you pay a monthly premium.

Long Term Care Insurance

Many government employers provide access to long term care insurance coverage.

The insurance premiums are completely paid by the employee. Premiums are based on a person's age at time of application.

Long term care insurance covers chronic illness, frailty of old age, or a serious accident. Care may be provided at home, in an assisted living facility, or in a nursing home.

Government employees and their eligible family members (i.e., spouses, parents, parents-in-law, step parents, adult children, adult siblings - including stepbrothers and stepsisters - grandparents, grandchildren, nieces, nephews, aunts, uncles, and in-laws between the ages of 18 and 79) may apply for Long-Term Care (LTC) insurance.

Long Term Disability Insurance

Long-Term Disability Insurance helps protect you from loss of income if an illness or injury prevents you from working for six months or more.

Many government employers offer Long-Term Disability Plans (LTD.) These plans offer insurance that covers:
- Replacement for a majority of your salary
- A guaranteed minimum
- Extra money for your children's education
- No offset for certain income
- Payments for partial disability
- Additional family care expenses
- A survivor benefit if you die while receiving LTD benefits

Legal Services

Many government employers offer a Group Legal Services Insurance Plan. This is a employee-paid plan that provides comprehensive legal coverage. It is intended for the most common legal need. It is completely voluntary; you elect to purchase this coverage.

The plan's covered services include, but are not limited to:
- Will preparation
- Domestic matters (divorce, separation, annulment)
- Bankruptcy proceedings
- Consumer protection
- Real estate transactions

- Defense of criminal misdemeanors
- Civil actions

In addition to services for covered matters, attorneys will review and prepare documents, give advice, and negotiate on the employee's behalf in any matter not specifically excluded.

Employee Wellness Programs

If you have an addiction, medical problems, legal issues, emotional disturbances, an addiction, stress related problems, marital problems, or other personal issues, the government will encourage you to voluntarily seek counseling. Most government agencies offer some sort of Employee Wellness Program that addresses these issues.

Employees are eligible for this counseling, as are their families (lawful spouse or registered domestic partner, and unmarried dependent children under the age of 23.)

Employee Wellness Programs typically offers several services, such as:
- Clinical Support
- Work & Life Services
- Financial Services
- Legal Services
- Identity Theft Recovery Services
- Daily Living Services

What these services actual entail varies by employer. It will usually include some kind of referral to rehabilitation if you are struggling with an addiction or disorder. It may include several sessions of free counseling. You may have access to a lawyer, referrals to in-home health care, a financial planner, and home-life balance assistance, such as a concierge service.

Some government agencies offer additional wellness benefits, such as discounts to local gyms, Weight Watchers, or Jenny Craig. Some agencies also offer their employees the use of free bicycles during work hours.

Vacation and Other Time Off

Vacation

When you first start working for the government, you don't get a lot of vacation time. After your first 3 years, your accrual rate increases. Below is a sample accrual schedule. Depending on exactly who your government employer is, you may have a completely different schedule:

Vacation

7 months to 3 years	7 hours per month
37 months to 10 years	10 hours per month
121 months to 15 years	12 hours per month
181 months to 20 years	13 hours per month
241 months and over	14 hours per month

Employers who offer vacation also typically offer 8 hours of sick leave per month.

Your employer may also offer annual leave. Annual leave can be used for either sick or vacation time.

Here's a sample schedule for annual leave:

Annual Leave

1 month to 3 years	11 hours per month
37 months to 10 years	14 hours per month
121 months to 15 years	16 hours per month
181 months to 20 years	17 hours per month
241 months and over	18 hours per month

As you can tell, you get less time overall with annual leave. In this example, you get 4 hours less a month than those who elect to get their vacation and sick leave separately. The only advantage of annual leave is that you can use it for any absence. Many people who get vacation and sick leave use all of their vacation very quickly, but build up large sick leave balances, which is useless unless you get sick. With annual leave, you can use all of your time for vacation – although you may be "docked" pay whenever you become sick.

As the years pass, you may find yourself accruing more vacation or annual leave than you can realistically use. Unlike many other places of employment, when you work for the government then you can "roll over" your hours from year to year.

Typically, once you have accrued six hundred forty (640) hours (or 16 weeks) of vacation time or annual leave, your HR department will contact you about a plan to start using this time. In most cases, you must start taking a day off each week until the balance has been sufficiently lowered.

Sick Leave

What exactly can you use sick leave for?

Sick leave is generally defined as the necessary absence an employee because of:
1. Illness or injury, including illness or injury relating to pregnancy;
2. Exposure to a contagious disease which is determined by a physician to require absence
from work;

3. Dental, eye, and other physical or medical examination or treatment by a licensed practitioner;
4. Absence from duty for attendance upon the employee's ill or injured mother, father, husband, wife, domestic partner, son, daughter, brother, sister, or any person residing in the immediate household. Such absence shall be limited to six (6) workdays per occurrence or, in extraordinary situations, to the time necessary for care until physician or other care can be arranged.

Holidays

Interestingly enough, paid holidays are not required in the United States. The Fair Labor Standards Act does not require an employer to pay employees for time that they don't work - including holidays.

Still, according to the Bureau of Labor Statistics, U.S. employees receive an average of 7.6 paid holidays a year.

But as a government employee, you get 9 official holidays. Depending on your union contract, you may get several addition "personal holidays" each year.

The government observes the following holidays:

January - New Year's Day
January - Martin Luther King Jr. Day
February - Presidents' Day

March - Cesar Chavez Day
May - Memorial Day
July - Independence Day
September - Labor Day
October – Columbus Day
November - Veterans Day
November - Thanksgiving Day
December - Christmas Day

Voluntary Time Off

Most government employees also have the option of getting additional time off – in exchange for giving up a small percentage of their salary. It's called the Voluntary Personal Leave Program (PLP).

You receive 8 hours of leave each month in exchange for having your pay reduced by 5%.

Only a small percentage of government employees seem to use this option, but the ones that do really seem to love it.

Family and Crisis Leave

One of the benefits of being a government employee is the time off that you get for family activities and emergencies.

Your union contract should have some sort of statement that says you are allowed to use your leave time (vacation, personal holiday, etc.) for the purpose of attending school or non-school family-related activities such as sports events, recitals, 4-H, etc., in which the employee's child is participating.

Your union contract should also address Family Crisis. It should say something like:

...employees shall be eligible to use accumulated leave credits for the purpose of dealing with family crisis situations (e.g., divorce counseling, family or parenting conflict management, family care urgent matters and/or emergencies). If the employee has exhausted available leave credits, the employee may request unpaid leave. Family is defined as the parent, stepparent, spouse, domestic partner (as defined in accordance with Family Code section 297), child, grandchild, grandparent, brother, sister, stepchild, or any person residing in the immediate household.

Sabbatical Leave

Many government agencies you to take an unpaid leave of absence for up to one year, with a guarantee that you may return to your former position upon return.

An unpaid leave of absence may be granted for, but not limited to, the following reasons:

1. Union activity;
2. For temporary incapacity due to illness or injury;
3. To be loaned to another governmental agency for performance of a specific assignment;

4. To seek or accept other employment during a layoff situation or otherwise lessen the impact
of an impending layoff;
5. Education;
6. Research project;
7. Personal or family matters
8. Run for public office

Mentoring Leave

Government employees may have the option for mentoring leave. This is up to 40 hours per year of special leave time to be used for mentoring activities (Girl Scouts, Big Brothers/Big Sisters, etc.)

Donation Leave

The government even gives you time off to donate blood or an organ.

If you are donating blood, plasma, platelets and other blood products to certified donation
Centers, you may be allowed reasonable release time without loss of compensation.

If you are donating an organ, you may be eligible for up to thirty workdays of paid leave.

Catastrophic Leave

Some government agencies allow you to receive "donations" of time off from other employees if you have a personal crisis in which you do not have enough time-off accrued to cover your absence, and you will go without pay if you continue to be absent from work.

For example, if you don't have a lot of sick leave but you become extremely ill or need surgery, other employees can give you their time off. Your HR Department will arrange the leave transfers and will deposit the time to your account.

Military Leave

Most government agencies allow you up to 5 years of military leave for active duty.

Here is a listing of the Government Military Code:

Upon presentation of a copy of orders for active duty in the Armed Forces, the National Guard, or the Naval Militia.... shall grant a military leave of absence for the period of active duty specified in the orders, but not to exceed five years...

A veteran who was reinstated from military leave shall receive layoff seniority credits for the time spent on the leave on the same basis as if it were service in the employee's former position.

You can take time off with pay to take a required physical exam before going on active duty.

If you're in the reserve military or National Guard, you can take time off without pay to attend scheduled reserve drill periods or perform other inactive duty reserve obligations.

If you're a permanent or probationary Government employee who gets called into service, you have the right of return to your former position. This can be:

- the last position you held
- a position at the same level
- a position to which you could have transferred

FMLA

The Family and Medical Leave Act (FMLA) allows eligible employees to take up to 12 weeks of unpaid leave during any 12-month period to attend to the serious health condition of the employee, parent, spouse, or child, or for pregnancy, or care of a newborn child, or for adoption or foster care of a child.

Parental Leave

Government employees may take unpaid parental leave.

Maternity leave is defined as:

A female permanent employee shall be entitled, upon request, to an unpaid leave of absence for purposes of pregnancy, childbirth, recovery there from or care for the newborn child for a period not to exceed one year. The employee shall provide medical substantiation to support her request for pregnancy leave. The request must include the beginning and ending dates of the leave and must be requested no later than thirty (30) calendar days after the birth of the child.
Paternity leave is defined as:

A male spouse or male parent or domestic partner, who is a permanent employee, shall be entitled, upon request, to an unpaid leave of absence for a period not to exceed one year to care for his/her newborn child. The employee shall provide medical substantiation to support his/her request for parental leave. The request must include the beginning and ending dates of the leave and must be requested no later than thirty (30) calendar days after the birth of the child.

During the period of time that an employee is on parental leave, the employee continues to receive their health, dental, and vision benefits.

Jury Duty

Government law does not require employers to compensate employees who are called for jury duty. One of the benefits of being a government employee is that the government will pay for you to attend mandatory jury duty.

You must provide your employer with a copy of the summons in order to get the time off.

Time Off to Vote

Government law allows employees who don't have enough time to vote during non-work hours to receive up to two hours of paid time off to go vote.

The Challenges of Government Employment

Will You Succeed as a Civil Worker?

You will encounter many challenges to obtaining a government job.

But before you even begin, you should make sure that you're up for the challenge. You should ask yourself a series of questions to ensure that civil service is the right kind of employment for you.

These questions are:
- Am I willing to fill out hundreds of applications to get this job?
- Am I willing to interview, many times, for this job?
- Am I willing to take a job that I don't want – just to get my foot in the door?
- Am I willing to take a smaller salary than I think I deserve?
- How will I manage the (conservative) work environment of a government office?
- How will I manage it if the work is routine and boring?
- Can I work with people that I may not like – and definitely don't respect?
- How will I keep from becoming resentful if my coworkers are lazy?

- Can I work with a boss who is a coward, or has another serious personality defect?
- Can I work with people who are toxic?
- How do I feel about being in a union workplace?
- Can I see myself working in a government office for 5 years? 10 years? 20 years?

The point is, there are plenty of government jobs out there. Getting one is really a numbers game. The more important question is: do you *want* a government job?

It should seem obvious – you do want a government job. That's why you purchased this book, right?

Many people are attracted to government employment for the job security, the generous benefits, and the pension. They rarely spend any time thinking about the downsides of government employment.

However, in order to move forward in the application process with the necessary enthusiasm and commitment – again, getting a government job could take a year or more – let's discuss the challenges of being a government employee.

If, after reading this section, you still feel 100% committed to the process, you will be lightyears ahead of other applicants. You've evaluated the pitfalls, thought carefully about what your future career will be like, and decided to pursue it with everything you've got.

Read through the following challenges and spend a few minutes thinking about how you would address these in your new career.

Once you're done, the following chapters will give you an overall guideline on how the civil service process works, followed by the specific steps necessary to obtain a government job.

Challenge #1: Why is the Salary So Low?

The first time that you open up a government paycheck, you may be shocked. If you've never paid union fees or a pension contribution before, you'll discover that a large percentage of your paycheck is missing. Pension and union contributions vary, based on a percentage of your salary, but it can easily amount to several hundred dollars.

On top of that, government work generally pays less the private sector. On average, government employees make 35% less than their counterparts in the private sector. On the bright side, your retirement and benefits are generally better.

Challenge #2: Why is There So Much Red Tape?

Working for the government is night-and-day different than working for the private sector. If you've ever worked for a corporation and felt like a cog in a giant machine, multiply that feeling by a thousand percent!

In the private sector, you understand what you were hired to do, but it's likely there will be many things you do over the course of your career that are a little different. You'll be assigned a new task you've never done before, or be asked to cover someone else's duties for a period of time, or take on special projects.

This doesn't happen in the government – at least not in the lower (non-managerial) levels of employment. Your job description is clearly outlined. Every duty that is associated with your job is assigned a percentage (20% of your job is handling inquiries from the public via email, telephone, and email, 10% of your job is filing, etc.) You are not supposed to do any duties which are outside of your job description; indeed, you are forbidden from doing so, as you will be working "out of class" (more on that later.)

Much like your job description, there are written policies and procedures for everything. All aspects of your job - from paperwork, projects, procedures, and the exact usage of your time – must be documented in paper form and approved by a higher chain of command. There is little room for autonomy, rapid turnaround, or change. Trying to work outside of this system will get you written up, or even fired.

The government agency that you work for – whether city, state, or federal - is part of an enormous system. This system has standardized procedures for *everything*. Many of the policies and procedures may seem out of date, unreasonable, or irrelevant – especially if they were created decades ago. You will probably find these policies to be constraining, irrational, and even ludicrous. Several of your coworkers may outright refuse to do work, stating that the work they are being asked to do is outside of their job description – and therefore, they won't do it.

The regulations that control how you work are meant to protect you from being unfairly treated or fired. However beneficial they may be, you will likely chafe at the restrictions placed on you.

Challenge #3: Why Do I Have to Act Like Everyone Else?

To succeed as a government employee, you should be invisible. That means that there shouldn't be anything unique or flamboyant about the way you dress, the way you speak, or your personality. You shouldn't stand out – not to your coworkers, your manager, or the public that you serve. If you have no filter and you use four-letter words, or you dress like the Tuesday Night Special, you will find that the government has little tolerance for this.

The government doesn't like attention-seeking employees, rule breakers, free-thinkers, unpredictable personnel, or workers who enjoy challenging authority. To succeed in government employment, you should be as quiet and predictable as you can.

This also means that you should understand the hierarchy – and not try to do things without clearing it with your supervisor first. Although technically an adult, it's like you've been sent back to grade school – you need to raise your hand for permission, first.

If you try to "fix" or "improve" upon a process by making it more efficient or changing the way it's done to something that makes more sense, you may be disciplined. Anything you do outside of your normal scope of job duties should either by a request initiated by your supervisor – preferably in writing – or something that you requested to do and received written permission from your supervisor.

All of your actions must be cleared first, or you will be reprimanded for acting without precedent, without approval, and outside the limits of the work that you are assigned to do. It doesn't matter what your intentions were. You didn't conform.

Challenge #4: Why Am I the Only One Doing the Work?

In government work, it is the ability to conform - not performance - that is rewarded.

You should do *exactly* what is required of you. You should perform the duties that were assigned to you in your duty statement. No more. No less.

Working too hard will turn other employees against you. If you approach government employment with the same zeal and efficiency that you put into private sector work, expect to be taken aside and told privately that you are "working too hard" and "making the other employees look bad." Perhaps you are responding to emails too quickly, or processing paperwork too quickly, or returning phone calls too quickly. Your efficiency means that members of the public will now expect this kind of efficiency from *all* other employees. Continuing down this path will make you an outcast.

My advice is to slow down. Act is you are participating in a time-efficiency study, and your job is to make sure that you're not observed working at an unsustainable pace. Your supervisor may act thrilled to finally have a hard-working employee who gets the job done, but the only thing that will happen is that you'll be assigned all the work that your coworkers refuse to do, and then no one will want to talk to you for being such a show off, too!

Remember: think grade school. Yes, it really is that petty. Don't set yourself up for failure – and cause your coworkers to undermine you because your good intentions are hurting them.

Challenge #5: Why Do I Have to Work With Idiots?

Unfortunately, as a government employee, you are likely to be surrounded by incompetent or freeloading employees. These employees are typically assigned very little work. The work that they do is often so poor that it needs to be redone by a more competent employee. Their contributions range from meaningless to harmful.

How can you spot these employees?

Here are some clues:
- They don't come to work on time
- They leave work early
- Their breaks and lunches last several hours
- They are always going out for a coffee, or they take a lot of smoke breaks
- They are AWOL in the middle of the day
- They're never at their desk when you need them
- Management has given up on trying to keep track of them
- No one cares what they're doing
- They talk and gossip nonstop
- They take personal phone calls at work

- They watch movies at their desk
- They put mirrors in their cubicle so they can see who is coming up behind them
- They constantly talk about how busy they are (but you never see them working)

Why aren't these employees fired?

Once you are hired by the government, it is virtually impossible to get fired. They may not have started out as bad employees. However, the constant drain of being surrounded by other employees that never do any work may have rubbed off on them. They may have been burned – overloaded with work that other employees refused to do – until they snapped, and then decided that they weren't going to do any work either.

Some of these employees may be likeable, friendly, funny, and seem helpful. You may enjoy their company – but resent how they don't actually help with the workload at all. I'll leave it up to you whether or not you want to form friendships with these types.

Challenge #6: Why Does My Boss Seem to Hate Me?

Working for the government means that your work will now be influenced by politics that aren't as big of a factor in the private sector. In the private sector, it's usually all about the bottom line. In the government, since there is no bottom line, it's all about control.

The government is filled with a lot of big fish in one little pond. All the fish are trying to one-up another. You may spend six months on a project that dies a sudden and merciless death because another manager doesn't believe that your project doesn't fit into their plans for what their goal is for the agency. Or, another manager throws you and your project under the bus because they want their own project to get the spotlight. If one manager decides that they don't like you, suddenly all of the people in their little department may become "unavailable" whenever you need their help. Or they may not have the "authority" to assist you with your work.

Politics are an inherent part of the job. Wise up to the political situation in your agency as soon as you can. Your best bet is to be as neutral as you can in the face of blatant power-mongering.

Also, be aware that local politics – such as the annual budget allotment for your city, or who is elected governor – may have an effect on your job.

Challenge #7: Why Do I Feel Like I'm Part of the Problem?

Most people are cynical about the government. Many view the government as part of the problem – not the solution.

When you work for the government, you're also seen as part of the problem. An extension of a bloated, overfunded, unhelpful machine.

You may be less respected by others than if you worked for a private corporation. There is a strong stereotype in existence that government workers are lazy – that they enjoy three-martini lunches and long strolls around government parks, rather than engaging in any kind of productive work.

As animosity for pensions grow, you may find yourself the target of much envy. Others believe that you are enjoying otherwise undeserved generous benefits, a ridiculous amount of holidays, and a wealthy retirement. As more people have begun to struggle financially, those employees lucky enough to have pensions have increasingly come under fire. Over the next few decades, you are likely to see more rhetoric calling for the abolishment of public pensions and for a reduction in government workforce.

No matter what your feelings about the size and limitations of government are, once you begin working for the government you will find yourself in the middle of a debate about the role of government. And to many people, you're on the losing side.

Getting Hired

How Does the Hiring Process Work?

The civil service application process is very different than the private sector.

In the private sector, you would typically find a job listing in the newspaper or online that you're interested in. You would send your resume to an individual or to an HR department, and your resume may be "read" by a computer program and not a live person. If you're deemed qualified based on what you put on your resume, you're invited for an interview. Your interview is likely to be conversational, with back-and-forth questions and answers. If you're the winner, your references are checked and you're offered the job. If you don't do well on the job, you're fired.

The government uses the civil service process. I have broken this process down into 6 steps, with an explanation of each one.

Step #1: Apply to Take an Exam

During your first step towards government employment, you will focus on:

- Understand what sort of work you are eligible and qualified to do for the government

- Locate the civil service name for the type of work you are eligible for (for example, a basic office clerk type job might appear under several different names: Customer Service Representative, I, Office Assistant, Office Technician, Motor Vehicles Representative I, Program Technician, etc.)

- See if there is the exam currently being offered

- If not, wait for the exam to be offered (can take up to 3 years)

- If it is, apply to take the exam by reading the exam announcement. If it is an internet exam, it will link you the appropriate website. If it is not an internet exam, you will need to fill out the government application form and any other required paperwork (such as a Supplemental Application) and send it to the contact information listed in the exam announcement.

- You will receive a letter indicating if you are qualified to take the exam, and if so, the date/time of the exam

Step #2: Take the Exam

- Take the internet exam

- Or, submit your written exam/list of qualifications

- Or, appear at the exam location at the government date/time to take an in-person exam

- Wait to be notified of the exam results

Step #3: Get Your List Results

- If you took an internet exam, you should be notified immediately of your score/results

- If you took an in-person exam, you will need to wait for the letter with your results

- Typically, if you scored in ranks 1-3, you are hirable

- If you did not "rank" high enough, typically you must wait one year to take the exam again

- If you have "ranked" high enough, you can begin searching for vacant positions for that exam classification only (for example, if you took the Office Technician exam, you may begin searching for vacant Office Technician positions. You cannot apply to any other type of positions, such as Office Assistant.)

Step #4: Apply for Vacant Positions

- Locate vacant positions that you are interested in
- Fill out the government employment application form and other required documentation (such as a Statement of Qualifications)
- Mail your application package or submit it via email before the final filing date for the vacant positions
- You will either get a letter stating that you are not qualified for the position, or you will hear nothing at all, or you will get an invitation to interview

Step #5: Interview

- You will have an in-person interview, typically with a panel of 3 people
- You may have a second interview as well
- Your references will be checked
- You will receive a job offer
- You accept the job

Step #6: Pass Probation

- Your work will be evaluated for the next 6 months to 1 year. You will typically receive 2 to 3 progress reports, and meet one-on-one with your supervisor to discuss them

- If your work is found satisfactory, you pass probation

- Unless you do something that seriously violates the norms of your work environment (watch anything X-rated on your work computer, become violent with a coworker, begin accepting bribes, have your family members hired to work with you in the same office, have your spouse's business accept a contract to do work with the government, etc.) you will never be fired from your job

The following steps are explained in more detail in the following chapters.

Step #1: Apply to Take an Exam

The exam is your first real step to getting a government job.

Why an Exam?

Many more people want government jobs than can have them. Government exams are designed to narrow down a huge pool of people who want government jobs into a small group of applicants who are certified as being "qualified."

Exams are the first step in the application process. They are a valuable tool that establishes a prospective applicant's eligibility.

For Human Resources and for the government, it serves as a qualifier. The exam ensures that applicants are qualified enough to do the job they will be applying for. It also is a filter that protects against personal bias in the hiring process (racism, ageism, etc.) Anyone can take an exam, as long as they meet the minimum qualifications.

For the applicant, the exam is a useful tool that narrows down the pool of prospective applicants. Instead of competing for a limited number of jobs against anyone who talks in off the street, they are only competing with other applicants who have taken and passed the exam.

How Exams Work

Exams are designed to test you. Depending on what position you are applying for, they may test you on any of the following: grammar, spelling, sentence structure, business writing, reading comprehension, alphabetizing and filing, basic clerical skills, basic arithmetic such as multiplication, division, addition, subtraction, fractions, decimals, graphs and tables, percentages, budgets, judgement, customer service skills, communication, or the ability to follow policies and procedures.

Civil service exams are rated on a scale of 100, with 70 and above usually considered "passing."

If you applied for a job that did not require a written test, your rating is based on the experience and training that you listed on your application. Examiners will determine what your score is, based on the information that you provided.

One of the most confusing things to people who are new to the civil service process is that not all exams are offered all the time.

You may be very interested in doing a particular job, but when you go to take the exam, you find that the exam is not offered. You may need to wait years for a particular exam to be offered.

Exams have "life cycles." Here is how it works:

The Life Cycle of an Exam

1. In a behind-the scenes examination, Human Resources of a particular government agency discover that they need more applicants for an exam list, or that an exam list is several years old, and a new list of qualified applicants needs to be created

2. The exam bulletin is released

3. Members of the public who are searching online for government jobs, find the exam

4. Those who want to take the exam submit government applications to the contact information listed on the bulletin. Any applications received AFTER the final filing date on the exam are deemed ineligible

5. Applications are reviewed by HR personnel to determine if the applicant meets the minimum qualifications for admittance to the examination

6. Applicants who meet the minimum qualifications are notified. They are given the date, time, and location of the exam

7. Applicants who do not meet the minimum qualifications are also notified

8. The exam is given

9. The exam is closed to new applicants

10. Several weeks afterwards (typically up to 6-8 weeks), applicants are notified by letter of their score and ranking.

Applicants with passing scores are added to the eligibility list

11. Applicants apply for jobs, citing their eligibility on the list

12. The Human Resources departments of various agencies access the list when they have vacancies without a high number of applicants, and send vacant positions announcements to those on the list

13. After a certain amount of time, the number of applicants on the list dwindle to such a small number, or the exam list is so old, that this prompts the "life cycle" to begin again

As mentioned above, once you have taken an exam you will (eventually) be notified about your score and/or rank. If you are in Ranks 1, 2 and 3, you are eligible for employment. The people in Ranks 1-3 may be hired if there is a vacant position that needs to be filled. If you scored in Ranks 1-3, congratulations!

If you scored below Rank 3, you must wait until the people in the ranks above you are hired. You will move up on the list as people vanish from the upper ranks.

Unfortunately, there is a possibility that you will not move up enough to see Ranks 1-3 before the exam list expires. The list typically expires every year – that's not a lot of time to move up. That is why it's so important to take several exams and to be on several eligibility lists at one time. This will increase your odds of getting a government job.

Unless you are getting a seasonal position, you will need to take some sort of exam in order to get a government job. It is a cornerstone of the civil service employment process. The exam is your first real step to getting a government job.

Types of Exams

Generally speaking, the government offers 7 different kinds of exams:

1. Written Test
2. Oral Interview/Qualifications Appraisal Panel (QAP)
3. Internet/Automated Exam
4. Performance Test
5. Supplemental Application/Achievement Rating Test
6. Education and Experience Evaluation
7. Agility/Physical Ability

Here is more information about each type of exam:

1. <u>Written Test</u>: A timed exam that consists of various job-related, multiple-choice questions that cover the knowledge and abilities needed to successfully perform the duties of the classification being tested. When you apply to take this exam, you will receive a letter with your test date, location, etc.

2. <u>Oral Interview/Qualifications Appraisal Panel (QAP)</u>: While facing a panel of two to three people, a candidate responds to predetermined job-related questions regarding education and experience, as well as situational/hypothetical scenarios. The candidate's responses are scored against a

predetermined list of suggested responses and benchmark scores that were developed prior to the examination by subject matter experts. This exam resembles a traditional interview.

3. Internet/Automated Examination: This is an online examination where a candidate responds to education and experience questions, or is scheduled to appear at a test site to take a computer-based test. It is typically a self-assessment. This type of test can be taken online. That means it can be taken by thousands of people, which results in extreme competition.

4. Performance Test: This type of test is primarily used for clerical and trades classifications. A candidate demonstrates their knowledge of tools and materials, or the ability to operate machines or equipment.

5. Supplemental Application/Achievement Rating Test: This examination consists of written answers to prompts, much like essay questions. For some agencies, the standard application serves as your examination, and there is no further testing component. More often, supplemental questions are added as an additional requirement to the standard application. The candidate indicates his or her level of knowledge and experience to predetermined questions, in addition to indicating the frequency at which they have performed specific job related tasks. A candidate typically completes this exam on his/her own and without supervision, then sends it in via mail. The responses are rated against a predetermined list of suggested responses that were

developed by subject matter experts and a Selection Analyst.

6. <u>Education and Experience Evaluation:</u> This examination consists of an evaluation of a candidate's application; no interview is conducted. It is a questionnaire which is scored. It rates a candidate's education and experience as indicated on the examination application against predetermined rating criteria. You will likely be asked to provide references who can verify the information about your education and experience that you have provided on your exam. You will rate your experience on performing specific job-related tasks and provide relevant examples. You will provide information such as your experience performing a task and relevant training directly related to the task.

7. <u>Agility/Physical Ability:</u> For law enforcement and other jobs, physical ability tests are given. They are frequently combined with vision and hearing tests. These are usually given just prior to hiring.

Finding an Exam

So, how do you find the government exams?

If you are searching for a federal job, then you will want to go to: https://www.usajobs.gov/

This is the federal government's official employment website.

If you are looking for a state job, county job, or a city job, find the official Human Resources website for that area.

No matter what kind of agency you're looking at, you only want to look for "open" exams – not "promotional."

What is an open exam?

It is an examination being administered for *any* interested party. Applicants do not have to be a government employee to qualify to take the examination.

"Promotional" exams are promotions for people who are already working as a government employee. They are not open to the general population.

How Long Do Exams Stay Open?

The minimum length of time that an exam can be advertised to the public is for 10 days. Some special exams may have a one-day, in-person filing period.

The more popular, entry-level exams, like Office Assistant, Office Technician, Account Clerk, and Program Technician, are typically "continuous file." That means it is an examination that does not have an established final filing date. It is advertised as an open exam, year-round.

On the other hand, some exams are only offered once every few years. If you have your heart set on a particular exam that is not currently being offered, keep checking the government jobs website weekly to see if the exam has been listed.

How to Read an Exam Bulletin

Exam bulletins are full of information. They usually include the following:

Examination Title – provides the classification name of the examination being administered. **Examination Base** – identifies the type of examination being administered and the type of list that will be established.
Who Should Apply – identifies who can apply for the examination and gives the limitation of the testing period for the classification, if applicable.
How to Apply – gives the location and address(es) where applications for the examination must be submitted.
Application Deadline / Requirements – gives the date (final filing date) when all applications must be submitted and the time by which applicants must meet minimum qualifications.
Test Date – shows the anticipated testing date(s).
Salary Range(s) – lists the beginning and ending salaries and lists any pertinent information that may affect salaries.
Minimum Qualifications – lists the minimum education and/or experience needed for the applicant to be admitted to the examination.
Examination Plan – describes the examination, the weight of each component, and the knowledge, skills, and/or abilities required for the classification being tested.
Additional Desirable Qualifications – if applicable, lists any special personal or physical characteristics or additional desirable qualifications that are deemed valuable for the performance of the job.

Eligible List Information – the proposed duration and type of employment list.
Position Description and Location(s) – provides a brief description of the responsibilities and duties of the classification and the location of current or anticipated vacancies and/or positions. **Special Testing Arrangements** – gives instructions for those who request reasonable accommodation for taking the examination.
Veterans Points / Career Credits – in some examinations, veterans preference points or career credits are added to a candidate's final score.
Special Requirements – if applicable, provides information on peace officer requirements and classifications (some medical and records classifications) for which background investigations are required.
General Information – describes general information about civil service laws and rules pertaining to examinations. This information includes the competitor's responsibilities in the examination process.
Testing Information – gives telephone numbers to call for testing information.
Contact Information – the name of the agency and the phone number that you can contact if you have any questions.

If you have any questions about the exam being given, contact that agency through the phone number listed in the Contact Information section.

How Will I Know What Exam is Being Given?

Read the entire examination bulletin. At least one section will explain what type of examination will be administered

(e.g., Written Test, Qualification Appraisal Panel, Qualification Assessment, etc.)

It will also explain the scope of the examination. The scope identifies the knowledge, skills and/or abilities required to be successful on the job. It is very important that you are familiar with the knowledge, skills and/or abilities of the classification because these things make up the basis for the examination questions.

Am I Qualified to Take the Exam?

Before you apply to take an exam, you need to make sure you meet the minimum qualifications. In particular, you need to make sure you meet the experience and education requirements.

It can be helpful to know how the government defines experience and education:

Experience Requirements
Experience is defined as: the equivalent to full-time work, typically defined as 40 hours a week.

If you work part time, your work experience will be pro-rated, based on the number of hours you work.

Education Requirements

Equivalent to completion of the twelfth grade is defined as completing any of the following:
- Graduation from high school
- Passing the a High School Proficiency Test

- Passing the General Educational Development (GED) Test

Equivalent to graduation from college is defined as: Bachelor's degree.

An AA (Associate of Arts) degree does NOT meet this requirement.

Specialization in, or, major work in is defined as: Bachelor's degree in that field, or, show completion of course work in the field sufficient to constitute a major.

Possession of a master's/doctorate degree is defined as: completion of a graduate or doctoral program.

Honorary degrees do NOT meet this requirement.

Applying to Take the Exam

When you first look at an exam bulletin, it may not be immediately obvious how you can take the exam.

If you are looking at an exam bulletin online, look for a line that should read something like this:

CLICK HERE FOR AN OFFICIAL COPY OF THE EXAMINATION BULLETIN AND TO TAKE THE EXAM.

Depending on the type of exam, you may need to create an online profile in order to apply.

For other exams, you can apply by mailing a standard government application directly to the person/agency listed on the exam posting.

The standard government application will differ depending on whether you are applying for a city, state, or federal position. Typically, it will be called something like: Government Application Form for Examinations and Employment.

Do **not** send a resume in place a government application form – it will not be accepted! Government application forms are required as part of the civil service process; it allows everyone's application to be equal and does not confer an unfair advantage. (After all, not everyone is capable of creating a highly stylized and professional looking resume!)

Government applications are typically available in one of three ways:
1. Hard copy (paper)
2. Electronically (PDF)
3. Online through some a government online application system (Career Portal)

A standard government application requires you to fill out your personal information, basic employment history, education, work history, and demographic data.

If you mail your exam application rather than applying online, make sure the envelope is postmarked no later than the final filing date.

What If You're Not Admitted to the Exam?

If you apply for an exam and you receive a letter that says you are not qualified to take the exam, you can challenge that decision.

Appeals must be submitted to the Human Resources Director within 5 business days of the postmark date of the written notification. That means you must respond <u>immediately</u>.

Write a letter stating why you are qualified to take the exam. You could point out the accomplishments listed in your application, or even supply a new copy of your application with the relevant parts highlighted. Send any additional information that you may have overlooked about why you believe you are qualified to take the exam.

The decision of the Human Resources Director is final.

Tips to Filling out the Exam Application

- Do not fill out each application by hand. Between exams and vacant position postings, you will likely be filling out hundreds of these in your search for a government job! Save the application to your computer or to a flash drive. Type in your information, then save it as a PDF. Once you have a basic version that you are satisfied with, you can make small changes as needed. You can even save different versions of it – one for Office Assistant positions, one for Office Technician positions, etc.

- The most important part of the application is the employment history section. This is where Human Resources will look to determine if you meet the minimum qualifications. Your work experience in these sections should have the same keywords that appear in the job classification for which you are applying.

- How do you find keywords to use on your application? Get out the job classification, get a highlighter, and begin highlighting key terms and keywords that appear in the description. A good rule of thumb is that at least 70% of the key terms that you identify should also appear in your application.

- If you are eligible for Veteran's Preference Points, this is the time to say so. Veteran's Preference Points are awarded in all examinations administered on an open basis to all Veterans meeting the criteria.

What kind of points are awarded for veterans? It's typically:
- Veterans (10 extra points awarded)

- Widows/Widowers of veterans (10 extra points awarded)
- Spouses of 100% disabled veterans (10 extra points awarded)
- Disabled veterans (15 extra points awarded)

Internet Exams

Almost everyone who applies for government employment ends up taking at least one internet exam. It is the easiest exam to take.

Internet exams are typically multiple choice tests. They have a series of questions and multiple choice answers in which you will self-certify your experience.

Here are some examples of multiple choice answers that you can select from when you are taking an internet exam:

a. I have more than 3 years experience performing this task
b. I have 2 to 3 years experience performing this task
c. I have 1 to 2 years experience performing this task
d. I have less than 1 year experience performing this task
e. I have no experience performing this task

a. I have performed this task as an expert or I have trained others on this task
b. I have worked independently on this task

    c. I have worked under a supervisor's direction or assisted with this task
    d. I have not performed this task

    a. I have experience performing this task through my college experience
    b. I have experience performing this task through my work experience
    c. I have experiencing performing this task through both my college and work experience
    d. I have no experience performing this task

When you are taking an internet exam, if you can truthfully pick the answer that gives you the best score possible ("I have more than 3 years experience performing this task"…"I have performed this task as an expert or I have trained others on this task"…"I have experience performing this task through both my college and work experience"…) then pick it! The more that you indicate that you have experience and proficiency on a task, the higher your exam score will be.

Qualifications Exams

If you applied for an in-person type of exam, such as a Qualifications Appraisal exam, you will get a letter notifying you of the date, time, and location of your scheduled exam. It will also tell you what, if anything, you need to bring with you. Notifications of acceptance to an exam are generally sent within one month after the final filing date.

Despite the fancy title, a Qualifications Appraisal is just like an oral interview. A panel will ask you some pre-determined job-related questions.

The panel typically consists of a chairperson and one or two government service representatives, such as an HR person. For some open exams, a member of the public who is an expert in this field may participate. The chairperson represents the government and ensures the interviews are conducted in a fair and legitimate manner. The government service representatives are usually one or two levels above the classification, and they have knowledge of the classification being tested.

The goal is to evaluate how well your experience, education, and personal qualifications have prepared you to perform the duties of the classification.

The interview questions are developed from the knowledge and ability section in the classification specification and examination bulletin. All questions used in the exam are developed by subject matter experts familiar with the classification.

Qualifications Appraisal interviews are structured so that every applicant hears exactly the same question. The panel cannot rephrase or clarify any of its inquiries; however, it can repeat the question.

There are two types of Qualifications Appraisal interviews: patterned and structured.

1. Patterned Interviews
Competitors appear before a panel of two or more evaluators who ask predetermined questions, evaluate

competitors' responses, and assign ratings based on previously defined rating criteria.

2. Structured Interviews

Prior to appearing before the interview panel, competitors are given a specified amount of time to prepare responses to predetermined questions or problems. A competitor's responses are discussed with the panel during the interview.

Your responses will be rated in quality by the panel. Your answers will be compared to the answers of other candidates in the examination. Successful candidates are scored in order, with the most qualified at the top of the list.

Here are some tips to prepare for the Qualifications Appraisal interview:

- Dress appropriately.
- Take the time to read all the interview instructions you receive.
- Never complain about such things as "the system" or "management" or "my supervisor."
- Answer questions in terms of what is good for the agency, and for the government as a whole.
- Don't talk too long. If the panel has heard enough, they will change the subject. If you're unsure, ask the panel whether you should continue with the subject matter.
- If possible, you should make it known that you are a person who follows established policies and procedures. When in doubt, say that you would follow the chain of command. The government does not appreciate a "loose cannon."
- If there is a break between the questions – relax. The panel members are probably just catching up on

their note-taking. The more notes they take, the better you are doing.
- At the end of the interview, the panel will ask if you have anything you'd like to add. This is the time to present any additional information that you believe is important, or to reiterate something that you would like to emphasize. Or, if you feel you did poorly on a question, this is the time to revisit it.

Disability Accommodations

Do you have a learning/reading/physical disability? Do you need accommodation for the exam? The government provides reasonable accommodation.

Each agency is required by federal and government laws to provide Reasonable Accommodation (RA) under the following circumstances:
- When a job applicant or employee with a disability needs assistance in order to complete a selection process
- When an employee needs accommodation to perform the essential functions of a job
- When an employee needs accommodation to complete required training
- When an employee needs accommodation to benefit from employer-sponsored events

Employers are obligated to provide this accommodation, unless to do so would cause them undue hardship.

If you have a disability and/or need special testing arrangements, you will be able to request a reasonable accommodation during the filing and self-scheduling process.

The person who will assist you is the Reasonable Accommodation Coordinator of the department; if there is no such person employer by the department, than the EEO Officer will assist you.

Step #2: Take an Exam

As previously mentioned, there are many different kinds of exams.

The more popular exams such as Office Technician, Program Technician, and Staff Services Analyst, are typically available online. Some other exams require you to fill out more information about your educational, experience, or to answer supplemental questions. And finally, some exams are structured like an interview – where you appear in person and answer questions.

One of the most important things you can do when it comes to taking an exam is to just apply and get started. Don't wait until the perfect time or until you have more experience. Just start where you are, and take the exams that you believe you are qualified for.

Exam Scoring

If you take an internet exam, it should be instantly scored. You should be able to find out your results immediately.

If you applied for a Supplemental Application Exam, Training and Experience Exam, or a Qualifications Appraisal interview, you should receive a letter within 1-2 months notifying you of your score.

If you took a written exam, you should receive your results by letter within 1-2 months.

Step #3: Get Your List Results

What Happens After You Take an Exam

Here is the process:

After you (and your competitors!) take an exam, an eligibility list is created.

If it is an internet exam, the list is updated constantly. If it is a non-based internet exam, that list is created 4 - 6 weeks later.

The results will list the names of all successful competitors arranged in order of the score/rank. (You will never see this list – it is for HR Managers only.)

When an agency wants to hire for a position, they can request a "certification" of this list.

This "certification list" will contain the names of the individuals who have indicated interest in working in that geographical location, their desired tenure (permanent or limited term), and their desired time base (full-time, part-time, or intermittent).

Eligible candidates will appear on the list in rank order.

You will either receive your scores via a letter in the mail, or online.

Some internet examinations provide the ability to retrieve examination results electronically. Your login ID and password will be required to retrieve exam results.

If you get your results by mail instead of online, you will receive a "Notice of Examination Results" letter.

The letter will look something like this:

GOVERNMENT AGENCY
HUMAN RESOURCES OFFICE
CAPITOL MALL
WASHINGTON, D.C. 20001

06/01/18

NOTICE OF EXAMINATION RESULTS
EXAMINATION DATE: 04/29/18

EMPLOYEE, FUTURE GOVERNMENT
1000 ANYWHERE WAY
WASHINGTON, D.C. 20001

YOUR IDENTIFICATION NUMBER IS: 722141

EXAMINATION TITLE(S): RESEARCH SPECIALIST I

CONGRATULATIONS ON YOUR SUCCESS IN THE EXAMINATION NAMED ABOVE. YOUR NAME HAS

BEEN MERGED ONTO THE EXISTING ELIGIBLE LIST IN SCORE ORDER. THIS NOTICE SHOULD BE KEPT FOR THE LENGTH OF YOUR ELIGIBILITY ON THIS EMPLOYMENT LIST. WHEN FILING VACANCIES, THE APPOINTMENT METHOD WILL GIVE CONSIDERATION TO INDIVIDUALS IN THE HIGHEST THREE RANKS.

FINAL SCORE: 90

LIST TYPE: OPEN

LIST LIFE: 24 MONTHS

LIST DATE: 05/01/18

INCLUDED IN THE FINAL SCORE:
SUPPLEMENTAL REPORT: PASSED

*VETERANS PREFERENCE: NO

OUR RECORDS SHOW THAT YOU WILL WORK IN THE FOLLOWING LOCATION(S):
ANY LOCATION GOVERNMENTWIDE
AND WILL WORK:
PERMANENT OR TEMPORARY – ANY TIME BASE.

APPOINTMENT SUBJECT TO:
VERIFICATION OF REQUIRED CREDENTIAL OR DEGREE

TO FIND YOUR CURRENT RANKING ON THIS LIST, PLEASE VISIT:

http://www.usajobs.gov AND CLICK ON MY PROFILE, THEN MY RANK – ELIGIBLE LIST DISCLOSURE. FIND THE RANK MATCHING YOUR SCORE FOR THIS EXAM ON THE ELIGIBLE LIST DISCLOSURE. THIS IS THE ONLY NOTIFICATION YOU WILL RECEIVE SO PLEASE SAVE THIS NOTICE.

* VETERANS ACHIEVING A PASSING SCORE ON AN ENTRANCE EXAM WILL BE PLACED IN THE TOP RANK.

Your Ranking

As mentioned above, after you have taken an exam, you will be notified of your score and/or rank.

If you are in Ranks 1, 2 and 3, you are considered "reachable" – meaning that you have scored high enough to be eligible for hire.

If you scored below Rank 3, you are not high enough to be "reachable." As the people in ranks 1-3 are hired and disappear from the upper ranks of the list, you will move up in ranking on the list.

Unfortunately, there is a possibility that you will not move up enough to see Ranks 1-3 before the exam list expires. The list is supposed to expire every year – although some positions are so rare in the government that the exam is only given every 3-5 years.

You should take several different exams and be on several different eligibility lists. That way, if you are not considered "reachable" on one eligibility list, you may be "reachable" on others. This increases your odds of getting a government job.

Challenging an Exam Score

Most exams require a minimum score of 70% for you to "pass." However, even if you get 70%, 80%, or even 85%, you may passed but you are still "unreachable." You need to be in Ranks 1-3.

For most exams, that means that you need to score in the 90 – 100% range to be "reachable" for jobs.

If you disagree with your exam score, you have a right to challenge it. Contact the Human Resources Department of the agency that gave the examination, and say that you want to open an investigative examination into the scoring of your exam.

Exam List Expiration Date

List life is typically for 12 months, but it may be extended for up to four years.

Information about the life of a list may appear in an examination announcement, like this:

Eligible List Information:
Names of successful competitors are merged into the list in order of final scores regardless of date. Eligibility expires 12 months after it is established.

New candidates are added to the list frequently. Names of successful competitors are merged into the list in order of final scores regardless of date. Eligibility expires 12 months after it is established, which means candidates may "age" off of the list at different times.

Any candidate who scored high enough to be placed in the top 3 ranks (score groupings) is considered "reachable."

If You Scored in Rank 1...

If you're in rank 1, then you'll be the first to get a job, right?

I hope you've been paying attention. The answer is no.

First of all, any department has the discretion to hire *anyone* as long as they are "reachable" – within the first 3 ranks on the list.

Second, the government must first work through a list of any government employees who were laid off before they can hire from the "outside."

Another thing that can affect your scoring is Veteran's Points and Career Credits. (Veteran's Points have been in a previous chapter.)

Career Credits are extra points awarded in Open examination to current employees meeting the specified criteria. These are additional points that are added to a candidate's passing score.

With these additional points, those with Veterans Points and Career Credits can artificially inflate their scores to be above 100. You may have scored 100 on the exam and still be in Rank 3. Or you may have scored 95 and be in Rank 5. Those with Veterans Points and Career Credits are in the ranks above you with artificially high points.

Don't worry. These ranks shift constantly as the upper ranks are emptied. You may quickly find yourself in a higher rank.

Even if you are in Rank 1, don't assume that government agencies will be beating down your door to hire you. A lot of people in Rank 1 wait for someone from the government to contact them and offer them a job.

You are unlikely to ever hear from the government, except for the occasional "employment inquiry" letter sent out for a hard-to-fill position. You need to be proactive and contact the government yourself about vacant positions that you find.

What's an "Employment Inquiry" Letter?

Once you are on a eligibility list, you may receive letters for hard-to-fill jobs. Contact letters are sent to those who are reachable on the list.

If the eligibility list has more candidates than are needed for interviews, a random computer selection is used to choose the candidates that will receive a job inquiry. As a result, not all candidates in a reachable rank will receive a contact letter for every vacancy.

However, as candidates respond to the contact letters (whether interested, not interested, or not responding), candidates in the lower ranks move up the list.

You should be aware that failure to respond to the contact letter makes you "inactive" on that employment list. It is very important to respond to the contact letter, even if you are not interested in that particular job.

You are not required to interview for every job that you are contacted about, or to even accept a job after the interview, but you are required to respond.

You can decline a particular notification – known as a waiver – and remain on the list, but after three waivers, you will be removed from the list.

Step #4: Apply for Vacant Positions

Once you have received your exam results and you know you ranking, you can begin applying for vacant positions.

But first, you should know that you can only apply for positions that *exactly* match the name of the exam you took. For example, if you took the Office Assistant exam, you can only apply for Office Assistant positions. You cannot apply for Office Technician positions.

Depending on what level of government service you're applying for, you may be able to job search through a Career Portal (for example, federal jobs, state jobs.)

Using this portal, you can usually search by:
- Keyword
- Department
- Job Category
- Job Title (Classification)
- Geographical Location
- Work Type (Permanent, Limited Term)
- Work Schedule (Full-Time, Part-Time, Intermittent)
- Salary Range
- Other job classes that will be considered for the position
- Date that the posting was published
- Final Filing Date

Job seekers generally like to look for jobs in their own geographical area first, followed by the job title, full time vs. part-time, etc.

What's on the Application?

No matter what government agency you're applying for, most standard government applications ask for similar information. Information such as:

- Name
- Mailing address
- Work phone number
- Home phone number
- Job title for which you are applying
- If you need reasonable accommodation
- If you are currently employed by the government before
- If you have ever been fired, dismissed, or terminated
- If you have verbal or written fluency in any other languages
- Your typing speed (for typing applicants only)
- If you meet the age requirements (for select positions only)
- If you possess a driver's license (for select positions only)
- If you graduated from high school or have a GED, or the highest grade you have completed
- Educational history
- Employment history

- Signature line and date
- Survey of your age, gender, race, disability, and military history, for Equal Employment Opportunity purposes

Filling Out the Application

Once you find a vacant position that you are interested in, you will apply for it by submitting an application through an online portal, or submitting a hard copy through mail, or even dropping it off at the HR office of the agency that you're interested in applying to, if it's local.

Tips for filling out the application:

- Read through the job description and duty statement for the vacant position. Make note of any keywords. Use these keywords in the "Employment History" section to describe your work in a way that matches what they are asking for in the job description.

- Put the position number for the vacant job in the "Examinations or Job Titles for Which You Are Applying" field. Don't just put "Office Clerk" or "Information Technology" or whatever. Some large agencies advertise for and hire for several positions at the same time. You have to tell them exactly which position you are interested in, or your application may be disregarded.

- Staple a copy of your list results letter to the application. This saves the HR person to having to check for the results manually. Anything that makes their job easier works in your favor.

- Only put in job history which relates to the position you are applying for. That includes positions from 10, 15, or 20 years ago. Because you are not worried about age discrimination with a government job, you do not have to limit yourself to the past 10 years of job history in order to make yourself appear younger on paper.

- Resumes, cover letters, and letters of recommendation are optional.

- I recommend creating a general, completed application which you save as a PDF. You will probably be sending out dozens, if not hundreds, of copies of this form. Having a completed, basic copy with all of your personal information, education, and employment history will give you a good base from which to work from. Then, all you need to do is change the position number and the keywords for each new copy you send out.

- Providing your Social Security number on the application is optional.

- The application may ask if you have ever been fired. If it does, you must answer this question. If you have been fired, you have a chance to explain what happened in the "Explanations" section. Answer the question briefly and consider keeping it vague. You can use terms like "miscommunications" or "ethical disagreement" or "expectations were not clearly communicated" or "lack of direction from management."

- You only need to fill out the age requirements section and indicate whether you have a valid driver's license if the job you are applying for requires it. These are typically jobs for the prison or police,, where you may be physically interacting with inmates or driving them around, or accessing another government vehicle.

- Include official transcripts, certifications, and typing certificates only if they are required by the job posting.

- Don't forget to sign and date the application!

- Submit your application before the final filing date.

- Make or save a copy of the application for your own records. That way, if HR has any questions about your application, you will know exactly what you sent them.

Proofread Your Application

One of the best things you can do before submitting your application is to give it a final proofread and ensure that you are coming across as the best possible version of yourself.

Your application is a paper representation of yourself. It is important to demonstrate, from the first point of contact onward, that you will not be a problematic employee.

The best way to demonstrate this is to make your application easy to read for the HR manager who will encounter it. Show that you are a clear communicator.

That means your application should:
- Include appropriate keywords
- List your credentials
- Zero misspellings, missing words, grammar errors, and typos
- Has examples of experience directly related to the job description
- Shows "results oriented" experience
- Explains your experience in layman's terms (no abbreviations, acronyms, or technical jargon)
- Don't give the HR person too much to read. Why? You don't want to overwhelm the manager. He or she may have received hundreds of applications for this position. If they don't find what they're looking for in 20 seconds, you're not going to get a call back.

Cover Letters and Resumes

Should you send a cover letter?

A lot of advice you hear recommends that you always send a cover letter. But for a government position, all applications are expected to be treated equally. That means they may disregard your cover letter completely, and go straight to the application, in order to treat everyone in a fair manner.

Here's one exception. If you are substituting work experience for education, include a simple, short cover letter that explains this. This makes things clearer for the HR manager. But remember, do not give the HR manager too much to read. You don't want to overwhelm them. Keep it short.

A resume is standard and gives more information about your background. Although it is not necessary, almost everyone includes one. Include one if you have one – and if you don't, don't worry too much about it. You will most likely be judged by your application, and your application alone.

Submit Your Application

Here's one last additional tip: you should submit your application by mail, if you can.

Why? First of all, many government agencies only accept mailed applications, or they have a strong preference for mailing applications. If given a choice between submitting your application online and mailing it, you should mail it.

Second of all, if you submit it online, then that means that your application is likely to be printed by the HR manager. This is something you can't control. Who knows what your application is going to come out looking like on their end?

For example, what if:
- What if their ink is running out of toner?
- What if they print the wrong number of pages, leaving out one of the pages of your application?
- What if they staple them in the wrong order - making them think that your application is incomplete?
- What if they forget to print your application?
- What if there is a system error and your application appears in an unreadable format?
- What if there is a system error and your application is deleted?
- What if there is a system error and your application comes in with an ineligible time stamp?

If your application is going to end up being printed anyway, doing it yourself gives you full control over how the final product appears.

Furthermore, many online web forms only recognize simple text. That means if you used modern features in your application (bullet points, bold, icons, etc.) it won't look right on their end. What if it prints out as off-center, cuts off text, or comes out as special characters?

The system could have glitches and your application could come across as incomplete. Why take that chance?

Of course, your application could also get lost in the mail – but I think that the odds of an electronic system malfunction are higher than your application going missing.

Mailing it also allows you to include extra documents – such as a copy of your transcripts, a resume, and a cover letter (if you choose.)

Step #5: Interview

Do not expect to receive an interview from your government agency of choice right away.

Several weeks may elapse from the time you sent your application until the time that you get called for an interview. Remember, HR may have dozens, if not hundreds of applications that they need to go through, in addition to yours.

If it has been more than a month since the final filing date and you are very interested in a particular person, you can call the contact person listed on the job announcement to verify the current status of your application.

When you do get an invitation to interview, you should make sure you get the following information from the person who has called or emailed you:
- The name of the caller
- The name of the agency
- Confirm the job title (if you applied for more than one job at this agency)
- A phone number that you can call back in case there is an unanticipated problem or emergency and you should need to cancel the interview
- A copy of the duty statement (if you don't already have it)
- What the interview format will be (written portion, panel, etc.)

- Time/date of the interview
- Exact location
- The parking situation around the agency
- Anything that you may need to bring (copies of your resume, your application, a pen, etc.)
- The names and job titles of the people that you will be interviewing with – get the exact spellings!
- How long your interview is expected to last (this will help you anticipate whether to pay for 2-hour parking or longer)

Before the interview, you will want to review the information listed on the job posting and the job duty statement, if there was one. The Job Description and Duties and Special Requirements sections of the vacancy announcement will give you an idea of what some of the interview questions may be.

Also, look at the agency's website. Go to their "About Us" page or "About the Agency" page or "Press/Media" page to get an overview of the kinds of services and programs the agency engages in. If you know what department the vacancy is in – it may be listed in the vacancy announcement under the Department Information or Contact Us sections – try to find that department's webpage online and read it.

The day of the interview, make sure that you arrive early. Many government agencies are located in a busy, downtown area. Street parking is usually metered, and lasts

1-2 hours. Consider parking in a parking garage. It will be hard to concentrate on your interview if you need to move your car, or you're worried about a parking ticket.

Expect your access to a government agency to be restricted. Most government agencies, unless it is a small field office, have a security protocol that you need to go through in order to access Human Resources. You may need to speak to a security guard, sign in, wait for someone from Human Resources to come out to the lobby of the building to retrieve you, or wait for a security guard to call someone from Human Resources and then give you "buzz through" access. Allow an extra 5-10 minutes to get through security.

What a Government Job Interview is Like

Government job interviews are almost always panel interviews. If you have always worked as a lower-level employee, you may have never experienced a panel interview before. They are typically reserved for higher-level positions and for managers, to ensure that potential candidates get along with an entire team or several managers before they are hired.

Government interviews typically have a panel of 3 people doing the interview. At least one of the people will be from HR. Another one of them is likely to be your direct manager. The third person works in a similar position (a future coworker, a senior lead, or someone in a related position within the agency who you will work closely with.)

Being interviewed by a panel of people is advantageous for several reasons.

One, each person assigns you a score for your overall interview. Although you may score very poorly with one person, you may score very highly with another. This helps balance your score out.

Two, having more people on the interview panel also reduces the chance of bias. The panel member cannot say to the other panel members: "I just didn't like him. He rubbed me the wrong way." Instead, they must justify in concrete, viable reasons why they gave you a poor score.

Three, if you did not answer a question very well, having more people on the panel increases the odds that one of the panel members will speak out and say that they did not understand your answer very well, or that they would like you to provide more detail. People are afraid of looking stupid, so if you were interviewing with one person, they might just write off your answer if they didn't understand it. Interviewing with multiple people increases the odds that you will be asked for clarification, and you will end up giving a more satisfactory interview.

Once you are seated, ready, and after the introductions have been made, the interview will start.

You will be asked between 4 and 6 questions which have already been pre-selected by the interview panel. The questions will be on a piece of paper that is placed in front of you, and the panel will also read the questions allowed. That way, you will be able to both read and hear the questions and will fully understand them.

Every candidate who interviews for the position will get these exact same questions. This eliminates the possibility of bias.

Clean Up Your Digital Image

Before you go on the interview, Google yourself. Pretend that you're a hiring manager. In fact, pretend that you are a hiring manager who is deeply paranoid that a questionable joke, inappropriate picture, or strong religious and political affiliations on your social media is going to lead to sexual harassment/discrimination/alienation from peers in the workplace.

Remember, you'll be working for the government. When the government gets sued, their lawsuits can mean enormous payouts. They don't want to hire employees who might end up offending someone!

Is there anything questionable about your "digital self"? Anything that would cause a hiring manager to question how well you would fit in with the rest of the team?

If so, take the offending material down. If you can't take it down yourself, contact the webmaster or administrator of whoever owns the website. The sooner, the better.

Sample Interview Questions

These are the type of questions you may be asked:
1. An icebreaker - some variation of: "Tell us about yourself and your experience."
2. A question to gauge how you would work with a difficult coworker/manager/member of the public.
3. A situational question to verify that you understand the chain of command for dealing with potential problems, or problem people.
4. A question typically designed for insiders. An example would be: "Specifically, what legal resources utilized by this agency would you recommend to a member of the public who has questions about (insert scenario here)?"

If you are having trouble with a particular question, you are allowed to ask for clarification – but you are unlikely to get it. If the panel gives you any additional information about the question, or even rephrases it, it could be considered bias, since you are receiving information that the other candidates are not.

These are some other general questions that can help you with your government interview:

- Tell us about your experience and education that qualifies you for this position.
- Discuss an on-the-job mistake you have made, and how you learned from it.
- How would you deal with a difficult colleague or subordinate?
- How would you deal with a difficult customer or aggressive member of the public?
- What would you do if a coworker, or a member of your team, was not "pulling their weight" on a project? What steps would you take to resolve this issue?
- Tell us about a time you worked on a project with a team. What was your role, and what did you do to facilitate success amongst your team members?
- Tell us about a professional obstacle that you conquered, what the outcome was, and what you learned from this experience.
- Give an example of how you multi-tasked to complete several projects at a time.
- Why do you want to work for this particular agency?

Interview Tips

Here are some interview tips:
- Refer to widely understood standards of customer service

- Mention software that you know and utilize: Microsoft Office, Powerpoint, Excel, Publisher, Photoshop, etc.
- Convey to the panel that you are not a loose cannon, i.e. that you would not shout at or become abusive to a member of the public. Try to work a statement into your interview like this: "I would respect and adhere to the protocol and procedures as established by the agency when dealing with a member of the public or when fulfilling a Freedom of Information Act request..."

What is the Interview Panel Looking For?

As you answer your interview questions, keep in mind that the panel is looking for more than just information about your past experience and skills.

These are several "unspoken qualifications" that they are looking for, too. Here is a list:

- That you are literate, and you have a good command of the English language
- That you communicate professionally, and don't use a lot of slang
- That you will actually do the work that you will be assigned
- That you will continue to do the work you were assigned after you pass probation (i.e., strong work ethic)

- That you are capable of processing all paperwork associated with your job
- That you will not have unnecessary conflict
- That you will not challenge any managers
- That you will be polite to the public
- That you are not a "loose cannon"
- That you won't go to the media with perceived injustices
- That you are mentally stable, and without a drug/drinking problem
- That you are unlikely to have continuous "crises" or personal problems that will cause you to leave work or go AWOL
- That you will show up on time
- That you can work in a team
- That you will not get romantically involved with your coworkers
- That you won't reveal personal information about yourself that will make your coworkers uncomfortable (like that you visit a nudist colony on the weekends, or that you are licensed to carry a concealed weapon)
- That you can work with difficult people of all kinds
- That you won't try to change or overhaul the government work culture or system (hint: if you try, you won't win!)
- That you won't file a lawsuit or accuse anyone of discriminating against you

The Ideal Candidate

The above list mostly states what the interview panel is NOT looking for. So, what exactly in the interview panel looking for? Who is their ideal candidate?

The ideal candidate meets the following qualifications:

- Non-confrontational
- Gets along with coworkers
- Doesn't have conflict with managers
- Can interact successfully with the public
- Documents difficult communications via email (in case there's an issue later)
- Communicates using professional vocabulary
- Does not send personal emails (which can be read by the public using a Freedom of Information Act request)
- Doesn't gossip or chat excessively
- Can read up to and beyond a 6th grade level
- Doesn't use offensive language or ethnic slang
- Can do his/her work
- Won't complain if he/she has to do some of a coworker's work, too
- Does group work, serves on internal teams
- Shows up to work on time
- Doesn't take unauthorized breaks and lunches, or "smoke breaks"
- Mentally stable
- Doesn't reveal too much personal information
- Doesn't fight back when a new policy/procedure is implemented

If possible, try to convey the impression that you meet these traits throughout the interview.

Ask a Question at the End

You will be asked at the end of your interview if you have any questions.

The short answer is: yes. You should *always* have a question. If you have no questions, it's like saying that you are not really interested in the job.

If you're not sure what to ask, these are some sample questions:

- Have there been any changes in (Name of Agency)'s strategic plan since it was written in _____?
- I saw in the news that your agency recently _____. How is the agency responding to this?
- The director of this agency recently made the comment that _____. How is this reflective of the agency's overall mission?
- How does this department fit into the overall organization, as a whole?
- What kinds of assignments might I expect for the first 6 months of the job?
- Please describe your training program.

- Does your company encourage further education? Do you have an upward mobility program?
- What is the atmosphere of this office? Slow, fast-paced? How is communication?
- If you offered me the job, how would you want me to do it differently than the previous person did it?
- What are some of the main on-the-job obstacles that I would need to address in this position?
- Would you describe the typical training program for this position? What are the opportunities for upward mobility?
- What are some of the biggest challenges facing your department?

What Happens After the Interview

After the interview, HR narrows the candidates to the top 3. They may even conduct a second interview, to narrow it down further.

Then they will conduct reference checks. They will also confirm the candidates' list eligibility before extending an official job offer.

You will figure out that you are a top candidate when one of your references tells you they were contacted.

The Reference Check

HR will be checking your references – no doubt about it. Thus, you should make sure that you choose your references well. Make sure they want to give you a positive review.

Any of the following relationships may be good candidates for a reference:
- Supervisors
- Coworkers
- Clients
- Vendors
- Business contacts
- Professors
- Teachers
- Mentors
- Commanding Officers
- Club leaders
- Advisors
- Coaches
- Pastors
- Volunteer Coordinators

These are the sort of questions your references will be asked:
- How long have you known…?
- In what capacity?
- Is…a team player?

- Is…capable of working without supervision?
- Is…punctual? Reliable?
- Is…organized?
- How are…'s technical skills?
- Give an example where… exceeded your expectations.
- Give an example when… handled a difficult situation.
- Give an example when…had a conflict with another person or situation.
- Are there any areas where you think that…will have trouble performing the duties of this job?
- Would you recommend…?

If You Didn't Make the Cut

There are many unfortunate reasons why you may not have been a top candidate. Here are a few of them:
- There is an internal candidate
- They are looking for a candidate with more "diversity"
- Nepotism
- The boss wants someone who is very similar to themselves
- You will be working with difficult coworkers or public and they don't think your personality is strong enough
- You will be working with very shy, non-aggressive people, and your personality is too strong

- They want a candidate that is just like the last person who had the job
- They want a candidate completely different than the last person who had the job
- Another candidate went to a more prestigious school than you
- You remind the boss of someone they dislike

Don't take it personally. Keep on applying, and you will have plenty more interviews.

How Many Interviews Does it Take to Get a Government Job?

Unless you are in a very specialized field and there are a small number of candidates on the list, you will probably have several interviews. Very few potential government employees get a position on their first try.

You may have 5, 10, or 15+ interviews before you get your first government job.

I don't want to discourage you, but it usually takes at least one to two years to get a government job.

Remember you're in it for the long haul.

Step #6: Pass Probation

After you have been selected as the top candidate, and Human Resources has verified your references, and your references have given you positive reviews, you will receive a job offer.

Congratulations! Before we talk about probation, these are a few common questions.

What if You Don't Get Offered the Job You Want?

If this will be your first government job, my advice is to take it anyway. Think of it as a temporary position. Once you have your foot in the door, it is easy for you to accept another government job. If you are already working as a government employee, it makes you a much more desirable candidate for other government jobs.

And once you accept another job, it will simply be a matter of transferring your paperwork, not bringing you on as a brand new employee. This is a much easier process for HR.

There is no limit to the number of times you can change government jobs – just be aware that your probation will reset to zero each time you start a new position.

Picking Your Start Date

Human Resources doesn't hold all of the power when offering you a position. There are a few things that you can negotiate, including start date.

Don't assume that you have to start on a Monday, or on the first of the month. The HR manager may want you to start at a certain time in order to make processing your paperwork easier, but you can bargain for an earlier or a later start date.

The earliest start date that I have heard of is two days after the job offer was made. The latest start date I have heard of is 2 months after the job offer was made.

Choosing Your Work Hours

You can also negotiate your work hours – your official start and end time of the workday. Unless you need to be at work for certain hours in order to cover a public desk or a phone line, you may be able to start as early as 6:30am or as late as 9:30am (in one case, I know a guy that started at 10am) and end work as early as 3:00pm or as late as 6:00pm.

Whatever you and your manager decide on, make sure that these hours are listed on the "Job Description" form that both you and your supervisor will sign once you start government employment.

If it's not on that document, then your hours are not official. It could cause problems for you down the line if you get a new manager who does not like your current work hours and immediately demands that you start coming in earlier, or later. Get your official work hours in writing!

What is Probation?

Once you have your first government job, you just need to pass probation in order to become a permanent government employee and keep your new job. Probation lasts for six months, unless you are in a professional or managerial position. If you are, then it will last for a year.

Probation is kind of like what tenure if for professors or teachers. Your work will be evaluated, you will meet regularly with your supervisor, and if you pass your probation without incident, you pretty much have a job for life.

During probation, you are evaluated on your capabilities to do the job you were hired for. You need to be able to demonstrate your ability to perform the job duties that you were hired to complete. Although the standards will be low in the beginning as you first learn your job, you must demonstrate acceptable progress and the capabilities to fully perform at the expected level in order to pass probation.

For the record, most employees pass their probation.

If your boss plans on failing you on your probation, it needs to be documented extensively, so that you cannot say you were discriminated against. You will know if you are passing probation. Your boss needs to specifically write out the ways in which you are failing in your job, and meet with your frequently (weekly, for example) in order to make sure you understand that you are underperforming. Your boss also must give you specific actions that you can implement in order to correct your performance.

The following are some tips to help you pass probation and help you acclimate to a government working environment:

Tip #1: Get Started Off on the Right Foot

As they say: first impressions are everything. You'll want to show your coworkers and boss that you want to get along with them, and that you don't want to upset the current balance of power in the office.
Here are some tips to help you make a good first impression:

- Have a humble attitude. If you have offended someone, say something like: "I'm sorry, I don't understand, I'm new. Do you think you could show me the correct way to do this?"

- Ask to see any existing manuals, procedure memos, lists of duties and responsibilities, etc.

- Only do the tasks that you have been asked to do. If you run out of work and you want to do more work, ask your boss for more. Don't try to do a coworker's job.

- Offer to cover breaks and lunches of the receptionist, if there is a public desk or public phone line.

- If your boss asks to know what you did each day, tell him/her. If they want an hourly accounting of what you did, tell him/her.

- Ask coworkers to check your work, to see if you did it correctly.

- If your coworkers invite you to lunch or coffee, go. If you decline, you may not get a second offer.

- It's also advisable that you take part in any office celebrations, especially when you're new. Otherwise, you may not be seen as having "team spirit" or as having bonded with the rest of your team.

- Don't talk much about your personal life, unless asked.

- Be polite to everyone – the student assistants, the retired annuitants, the security guard, the mail courier, etc.

Tip #2: Show You're Competent – But Not a Show-Off

Takes notes at your new job. Act as if you have been assigned to create a detailed manual or instruction book for all of your job duties. Management will be grateful – because this will help other employees to do your job when you are out of the office, and it will also be very useful for your replacement if you get promoted or find another job. It shows initiative without making anyone else look bad.

When you are assigned work, verify with your supervisor that you have completed the work to satisfaction.

Ask if there are any long-range projects that you can work on.

Do the things that other people don't want to do. Volunteer to help run the annual food drive or collect donations slips for the annual government employee's charitable campaign. Offer to help plan someone's retirement party. Sign the birthday cards that go around. Take notes during meetings and offer to share these notes with anyone who missed the meeting. Offer to write the annual report, serve on a committee, clean up the break room, and just generally make yourself useful. Don't make yourself useful just to your boss – you'll gain a reputation as a kiss-up – but make yourself useful to everyone in your department.

Tip #3: Keep Your Own Records

From the first day you start, you will want to make copies of any kind of paperwork you receive from Human Resources or from your boss. Copy anything that looks like an official document or has your position number listed on it. This includes documents such as:

- Duty Statement
- Health enrollment paperwork
- Leave request slips
- Timesheets
- Performance reviews
- Training requests
- Leave balance statements
- Automatic payroll deduction requests

Also, you will want to make your own personal documentation of any difficulties you have on the job, or with other people. Take extensive handwritten notes, documenting the date, time, who was involved, what was said, and what the outcome was. Print emails, make screenshots, and keep records as if you will have to one day present your records to the union.

This is to protect yourself. One day, you could have a coworker accuse you of sexual harassment, workplace bullying, or inappropriate behavior. Or you could have a boss accuse you of going AWOL or of insubordination. If you have a long, documented history of difficulties with this person, your side of the story becomes much more believable.

Tip #4: Assume You're Being Audited

While you are on probation, you should be careful about what you do during your working hours.

The internet is right there; virtually every government computer has access to it. Some agencies block websites such as YouTube, Facebook, and Gmail, and some agencies have complete open access.

When you start government employment, you will sign some sort of "internet acceptance usage" form that basically says the government has a right to monitor anything you do on your computer. 99% of employees are not disciplined for recreational internet usage. But you will want to be careful during your probation.

Also be careful not to take too many smoke breaks, long breaks, or excessively long lunches. You never know when a fellow coworker, who is a stickler for the rules, may report you to a boss for that.

Passing Your Probation

While you are on probation, your supervisor will fill out 2-3 probationary reports about your performance.

Your supervisor can only evaluate your performance as it compares to what is in your job description. So take a look at your Duty Statement and make sure that you are meeting all the obligations listed on it. As long as you are, you should have no problems.

In the event that your supervisor writes a negative report, you do not have to sign the report. A negative report means that you are in danger of failing probation. Contact the union for assistance.

Most government employees pass their probation. Once you are working as a government employee, passing your probation will be one of your lesser concerns as you settle into your day-to-day work. If you have serious concerns that you may fail your probation, contact the union.

If You're Having Problems on Probation

Most government employees do not fail their probation. However, if you think you might, begin documenting your experience immediately. Write down as much detail as you can about altercations or difficulties that you are having with your supervisor or your coworkers. Write down any problems that you are having with your workload. Write down dates, times, names, and exactly what was said.

Don't make it easy for them to fail you. Start filing grievances (see next section.)

File a Grievance

As a government employee, you have more protections than you would in the private sector. If you feel that your rights are being violated, the first action you can take is to file a grievance with the union.

What is a grievance?

This grievance procedure is used to solve employment-related complaints.

A grievance is a dispute of one or more government employees, or a dispute between the Government and an employee, involving the interpretation, application, or enforcement of the express terms of the union-negotiated contract.

The purposes of a grievance are:
1. To resolve grievances informally at the lowest possible level.
2. To provide an orderly procedure for reviewing and resolving grievances promptly.

At any point in the grievance process, you may be assisted by, or have the presence of, a union representative.

There are two kinds of grievances: informal, and formal. The first step is to try to solve the grievance informally.

In an informal grievance, an employee's grievance is discussed with the employee's immediate supervisor. Within a certain number of days, usually seven, the immediate supervisor has to give a response.

According to the union contract, if an informal grievance is not resolved to the satisfaction of the grievant, a formal grievance can be filed within a certain amount of time, such as in the next thirty days.

To move forward with a formal grievance, you must do the following:
1. Submit it in writing
2. Include a statement as to the alleged violation, the specific act(s) causing the alleged violation and the specific remedy or remedies being sought
3. If desired, request a grievance conference
4. File it with your Department Head

After you file a grievance, you and the other party have to meet within a certain numbers of days to discuss the settlement of the grievance.

If you can't find a solution, or if you're not satisfied with the decision, it only escalates from there. You can appeal the department head. The department head must respond in writing. If it's still not resolved, the Union has the right to submit the grievance to arbitration. From there, it escalates even further – to the Government Conciliation and Mediation Service or the Federal Mediation and Conciliation Service.

Weingarten Rights

Write this out and put it somewhere where you can find it in a hurry, because this statement could save your job:

"If this discussion could in any way lead to my being disciplined or terminated, I respectfully request that my steward be present at the meeting before I answer any questions. Without representation present, I choose not to respond to any questions or statements."

The above statement is known as Weingarten Rights.

Your Weingarten Rights are especially important in a situation where you have a supervisor who is targeting you, bullying you, or trying to get you fired. If you think you may fail your probation because of a biased or difficult manager, make sure you invoke these rights.

This is a full list of your Weingarten Rights:

• If you do not know why your manager wants to meet with you, you must ask your manager if it is a meeting that could result in discipline.

• You have the right to have a union steward present during investigatory interviews where management plans to question you in order to obtain information, and you have a reasonable belief that discipline or other adverse consequences may result from your meeting.

• If you want a steward present, you must ask for one.

• If your manager refuses to allow you to bring a steward, repeat your request in front of a witness. Do not refuse to attend the meeting, but respectfully decline to answer questions until your union representative is present.

• You have the right to speak privately with your steward before the meeting and during the meeting.

• Your steward has the right to play an active role in the meeting - the steward is
not just a witness. For example, your steward can request clarification of confusing questions and otherwise support and assist you.

• If your manager denies the request for union representation and directs you to answer questions without a steward present, your manager is committing an unfair labor practice and you have the right to refuse to answer. However, do not leave until you have been excused by your manager. Any discipline taken under these circumstances could be challenged as improper.

Personnel File

Your personnel file is a record of all documentation about your hiring and your work performance.

You can request that anything negative in the file be reviewed, removed, or that you be allowed to contest it. This will become important as you promote up and your file is repeatedly reviewed by interested parties.

Want to see your file? Upon request, your HR Department has to identify where your files are kept. Your personnel file will also contain an inspection log, showing who has accessed your file and on what date. Other employees may not access your file; only supervisors and other agencies that you are interviewing with.

There shouldn't be any surprises when you review your file. You should have seen all of the paperwork before. Before any material is placed in your file, the department head or designee must give you an opportunity to review the material, and sign and date it.

You can view your official personnel file during regular office hours. If the file is kept outside your work location – say, stored at another location - arrangements can be made to have you view it at your work location.

You can also request to receive a copy of the material in your personnel file.

If you're serious about promoting up, consider asking your supervisors to write positive letters about your work performance. You are allowed to insert your own supplementary material into your file.

Likewise, if there is something in your file that you do not agree with, you can insert a written response to any items in the file.

How long does material stay in your file? Especially negative material?

Material relating to an employee's performance will be retained for a period of time specified by each department. However, at the request of the employee, materials of a negative nature may either be purged after one year or at the time such material is used in a written performance evaluation.

By mutual agreement between a department head or designee and an employee, adverse action material may be removed. When an employee receives written documentation of a negative nature, the supervisor shall note in writing on the documentation the time frame it will remain in the file.

After Probation

Congratulations! Once you pass probation, you have a government job for life (unless you do something criminal, illegal, or morally reprehensible.)

What should you do after probation?

Many employees are satisfied to stay in the position they were hired in. Although it may seem ridiculous to you, some people choose to work as an Office Assistant or Office Technician for their entire 30 or 40 year career! Some people just don't want the responsibility of doing more.

Many others go on to the highest levels of management – pulling in six-figure salaries.

A government agency is one of the last few workplaces where you can get ahead without a college degree or formal education. Within 5 – 10 years of your initial hire, you may be able to double or even triple your salary.

I hope that you find working for the government to be an enjoyable experience, and that you enjoy having a "job for life."

FAQ

Am I required to provide my Social Security number on my application?

Providing this is voluntary in accordance with the Privacy Act of 1974 (PS 93-579).

However, your Social Security Number is required for purposes of granting Veterans' Preference Points and Career Credits, and to check for eligibility for promotional examinations.

Do I have to be a U.S. citizen to work for the government?

No.

Generally speaking, only a few government jobs (mostly peace officers) require U.S. citizenship.

However, you must have the necessary work visas and meet all requirements set forth by the Immigration and Naturalization Service to be eligible to work in the United Governments.

Can I use a college degree from a foreign country?

Yes, but the government only recognizes degrees from accredited educational institutions.

What is the minimum age that you need to be to work for the government?

Technically, there isn't one.

According to Government Code Title 2, Division 5, Part 2, Chapter 4, Article 2, Section 18932:

Any person possessing all the minimum qualifications for any government position is eligible, regardless of his or her age, to take any civil service examination given for that position, except as provided in this section.

The youngest government employee I have met was 17 years old – a young woman who had taken her GED at 16. She got a government job as an Office Assistant. Her mother, who worked as a government employee in the same large department as her daughter, helped her navigate the application process. I'll leave it up to you to ponder if there was any nepotism involved.

If age doesn't matter, then why does the government ask about age requirements, or if I possess a driver's license on the application?

These questions pertain to positions for the Peace Officer classifications. As the instructions in the application governments, you need to answer these only if the examination requires it. You can leave these parts of the application blank.

I was fired from my last job. Does that disqualify me from government employment?

Not necessarily. The application may ask a question such as:

Have you ever been fired, dismissed, terminated, or had an employment contract terminated from any position for performance or for disciplinary reasons? (Applicants who have been rejected during a probationary period, or whose dismissals or terminations have been overturned, withdrawn [unilaterally or as part of a settlement agreement] or revoked need not answer "Yes".) Refer to the Instructions for further information. If "Yes", give details in the Explanations section.

The government is interested in knowing if you have been fired or terminated, but they give you a chance to explain any misunderstandings or wrongful termination that you experienced directly on the application.

I have a criminal record. Do I have to put that on my application?

Some government application forms (those who have "banned the box") does not ask you to provide any information about whether you have a criminal record.

For example, California law typically prohibits asking an applicant about an arrest that did not lead to a conviction or a diversion program.

Additionally, an employer is prohibited from requesting criminal background check information on the initial employment application.

However, for some positions, you may be required to fill out Criminal Record Supplemental Questionnaire. These are typically for positions with law enforcement, Department of Corrections, or for positions working with children or the elderly or the disabled. For these positions, you will have to reveal more information about your criminal background.

Can I still get hired when the government has a hiring freeze?

Even when the government has instituted a hiring freeze, employees still get hired.

How is this possible?

I have worked for the government during several hiring freezes, and I have seen new people get hired all the time. If a government agency can prove that a vacant position is "mission critical" – that is, a particular government agency cannot perform its basic functions without having a person in that position, then it is approved.

Here is the wording from one government press release about a hiring freeze:

The order allows for limited exemptions, subject to the approval of the Governor's Office. It permits agencies to fill positions that are critical to public safety, revenue collection and other core functions, in cases where these essential duties cannot be carried out at current staffing levels. Examples include positions that provide hands-on patient support in 24-hour care facilities and those that respond to emergencies, disasters or other life-threatening situations.

I used to work for the government. Do I have to do everything that you say in your book?

If you were previously employed as a government employee and your government service ended either by:
1. Resigning
2. Retiring
3. Accepting another civil service position
4. Or, your position was a limited-term, temporary position and it ended with you being in good standing with your employer

… then you may be able to restate to your previous job classification without having to take another examination.

You may be permissively reinstated without having to take another examination to a classification and time base in your previously worked classification or into a class in to which you are able to transfer. If you wish to reinstate, it is your responsibility to seek your own job within government civil service.

You may be permissively reinstated without having to take another examination to a classification and time base in your previously worked classification or into a class in to which you are able to transfer. There is no time limit for permissive reinstatement eligibility. If you are eligible to reinstate, based on the reason(s) for your separation from Government service, you can request permissive reinstatement at any time. When you submit your application for a vacant position, you should indicate you are applying based on your permissive reinstatement eligibility. The department to whom you submit your application will determine if you are eligible for consideration

If your position ended because:
1. You were absence without leave (AWOL)
2. You were terminated for failure to meet conditions of employment

…then you are considered a person who was terminated for cause, and you have no reinstatement rights.

Before you can take another government exam, you must submit a request to the government agency in order to take the exam. They will require certain information from you – such as the reasons for your termination – before allowing you to take the exam.

I work/worked for a University, Community College, or K-12 system. Do I have to do everything that you say in your book?

Yes. Employees of educational systems are not a part of the civil service system. Therefore, they are not eligible to transfer into civil service positions, and must go through the process like all other applicants do.

The exam for the job I want is not open. Now what?

Although some exams are offered on a continuous basis, other exams are only given every once in a while - say, every 3 to 5 years. Typically, these are for positions that do not have constant turnover and for which this is a sufficient list of candidates from when the last exam was given.

The good news is, once you take the exam and get the list, you are likely to stay on it for several years.

Be patient. Be sure to check for an exam bulletin every week, and consider taking other exams and applying for other positions in the meantime.

I am moving, or otherwise need to change my information. What do I do if I am on an exam list?

Write to department that gave the exam and notify them of your change of address so that you can remain on the employment list and get job opportunity announcements.

Why didn't I get a letter from HR saying that my application for a vacant position was received?

Assume that for every posted vacancy, the HR manager receives anywhere from 50 to 200 applications. Sending a letter is a common courtesy that the HR manager chooses not to observe. They are too busy going through all the applications. Don't let it bother you, and send out your next application.

Why didn't I get a letter from HR saying that I have been turned down for an interview?

See above answer.

Will there be a second interview?

Second interviews are common, although some government jobs have just one interview. The panel will inform you at the end of your first interview if there will be a second.

I've had a lot of interviews and I haven't gotten a job yet. Why?

It's probably not you. There are a lot of additional factors that could be at stake here, such as:
- An internal candidate
- A candidate with Veteran's Preference Points
- A candidate who has previous government employment experience (a reinstatement)
- A candidate who has previous government (federal, city, county) experience
- A case of nepotism (those in power giving jobs to relatives, friends, or others with connections to the person in power)
- A lazy HR person who has not checked your credentials thoroughly or failed to supply the hiring panel with all of your necessary information
- Panel members or a hiring manager with a strange bias
- Panel members or a hiring manager who want to hire people that are just like them
- You may not be a good fit for that department/team
- The job you interviewed for may have become frozen or subject to another political process
- A bad reference

What if I just accepted a government job – and then I get an offer for an even better government job?

I suggest that you take the better government job. This is a shocking common occurrence. Over the years, I have seen new employees call in just days before they were supposed to start, or even calling the morning that they were supposed to start. They leave a message telling HR that they are accepting a better offer. I have also personally trained several employees who quit after their first or second week after accepting a better job.

This is a normal occurrence. Don't feel bad if you don't show up to a new job or quit after your first few weeks for a better offer. There will be no hard feelings – everyone understands that you have to take the best job available.

What is the union?

As a government employee, you will be represented by a union.

All members vote to either accept or reject the working contracts that are negotiated with the government entity that employs them (whether city, county, state, or federal.) These contracts include decisions on items such as:
- Wages
- Medical, dental, and vision insurance
- Retirement
- Working conditions
- Vacation and sick leave policies

- Health and safety in the workplace
- Career development and upward mobility

What are Career Credits?

Career credits are applied to the final score of government employees who have permanent civil service status (those who have successfully passed their initial probationary period). These credits raise your score in an exam.

If an applicant receives Veterans Preference Points, he or she cannot also receive career credits.

Why is pay listed by range? Can I get top salary?

Unless there is compelling reason why you should receive top salary, you will start at the very base of the salary range.

Potential government employees who meet certain qualifications – for example, potential employees who would have to take a pay cut in order to accept a position with the government - may be eligible to start at the top range. Everyone else starts at the minimum range. Don't take it personally – this is how the government prevents discrimination claims and shows that all new employees are treated equally – by starting them at the same salary.

When will I get a raise?

In government worker vernacular, raises are referred to as "step increases." This means that for your raise, you go up one step – from Range A to Range B, for example. You receive a step increase for each year anniversary that you are in government service.

You will stop receiving raises once you are at the top range. After that, you receive COLAs, which are Cost of Living Adjustments. These are typically 2 – 3% salary increases, which are negotiated by the union.

Will I lose my retirement if I leave government service?

You must have a certain number of years of service credit to be vested with the government retirement system. This is usually 5 or 10 years. If you leave before you have accrued the appropriate number of years of service, your options are:

- Elect to refund or rollover your contributions.
- Leave your contributions and interest in your account and receive a retirement benefit as soon as you meet the minimum retirement eligibility requirements.

About the Author

This book was written and published by an employee who has worked for the government – either city, county, and state – for almost fifteen consecutive years.

Printed by Amazon Italia Logistica S.r.l.
Torrazza Piemonte (TO), Italy